Women of the Bible vs. Women of the Twenty-first Century

Dr. Erdie Mae Roberts Hutchings

ISBN 978-1-0980-6275-0 (paperback)
ISBN 978-1-0980-6276-7 (digital)

Christian Faith Publishing, Inc.
832 Park Avenue
Meadville, PA 16335
www.christianfaithpublishing.com

Printed in the United States of America

Contents

Abstract

The goal of the project was to use a prayer meeting to bring prayer back into the school so that God's will could be done in Earth and in heaven by witnessing, living, learning, and ministering the Word of God.

The following were the objectives of the study:

(1) To know that it is the authority of Jesus Christ and the Holy Spirit of Jesus is why we are here. To realize that we are here under the authority of Jesus Christ and the Holy Spirit.
(2) To start doing God's work, by grace through faith.
(3) To wash oneself daily with the Word.
(4) To witness by attending church.
(5) To go to people with the love of God.
(6) To remind others that when God spoke something in one's life upon preparation, Satan will use the old guard to try to come against that person.
(7) To handle conflict with the Word of God.
(8) To relate Scriptures to people's everyday situations.
(9) To improve techniques for missionary work.
(10) To savor successes and limit failures.
(11) To spread the good news.

In this study, the teacher was employed at Hillpoint Elementary School from September 2008 to June 2009. When the teacher got to the common area, they called it "God's meeting place." She had increased her ministry outreach to include custodians, guidance counselors, teacher assistants, and parents. She considered the ministry very successful in every way except increasing the attendance of other staff members and principals. This study looked at the successes and studied the failures. This project has continued to this day (requested by the attendees), as this teacher challenged other members of the prayer group to knock on classroom doors and invited others to the 8:00 a.m. prayer meeting, Monday through Friday.

ACKNOWLEDGMENTS

A special thanks be to God for a departed godly mother, Nora B. Roberts, to whom this book is dedicated. She instilled in me God's grace and mercy at the age of five, as she led me to God's Word, insisting that it become part of my daily walk.

It is an honor to give God the glory for saving a wretch like me and giving me the God-given gifts of writing and communicating.

Thanks also to my husband, William Senior, my three children—William Junior, Yalonda, and Brandon Hutchings—for their encouragement.

I thank my pastor, Reverend Doctor Jerome A. Barber, for instilling in me how to study the Word and how to have a relationship with God.

I thank Dr. JoAnn Jones and Dr. Charles Stover, English teacher, the providence dean of students, and vice president of academic affairs, who tirelessly and professionally heeded God's Word when they had taken me on as a student. Dr. Jones knew before I knew it that God had a plan for my life, and she never gave up on me even when I could not understand what had been happening to me. She stated, "You would not be able to handle it if God revealed more than a tip of his plan to you."

Dr. Stover, it would not have been possible without your long hours of looking over my papers and your words of encouragement.

Introduction
Surveying the Schoolteachers

A. Introduction

If women of the Bible could speak to women of the twenty-first century, they would say those women need to tame their tongue so that they could realize who God was, concentrate on God, and evangelize the world rather than worry about church growth. They would state that the women of the twenty-first century should also respect the views of postmodern women. Women of the Bible would then speak on how God was sovereign being large and in charge of the universe. Those biblical women would attempt to go on in hope to direct the women of the twenty-first century to a road to eternity so that women of the twenty-first century would not relive the past as they continued to evangelize the world.

It was important for women of the Bible and women of the twenty-first century to communicate so that this important information revealed the power and existence of God could be passed down through the generations. The Bible revealed that God did exist! God is and God revealed through women of the Bible as well as women of the twenty-first century! He used women of the Bible to speak to women of today so that his will would be accomplished, so that he would be glorified.

A project teacher, Erdie Hutchings had been teaching at the Suffolk Public School District for thirteen years who wanted to put prayer back into schools. She realized that the school system still had not officially placed prayer back in schools.

Actually there had already been prayer in schools. It was that moment of silence that had been instituted in the educational system after 9/11 that introduced her to prayer in school. She wanted more. People needed to see her vision so that God would be glorified.

B. The Prayer Meeting

Teachers, principals, and parents all definitely needed prayer back in the school. The reason this nation was in the mess it was in as a nation was because of the Supreme Court's decision to take prayer out of school. Well, prayer was put back in Hillpoint Elementary School. This prayer warrior teacher started out with two colleagues, and the prayer meeting continued to grow with an average of thirteen to seventeen members. The group had gotten many new members, male and female, and the prayer warriors were determined. Several of the attendees knocked on other teachers' classroom doors offering them the opportunity to attend 8:00 a.m. prayer meeting, which was held Monday through Friday after October 2008. These simple spoken prayers bound many things that otherwise stressed minds could not have contemplated. Only one woman caused the courts to take God out of schools. What could a multitude of God's people, with God's help, do to get God back in our schools? This would be a continued ongoing project for such a time as this twenty-first century.

The prayer meeting facilitator sent out thirty-five questionnaires to her colleagues, and she got several answers verbally and some on the survey form, nineteen total. Ten questions were subjective answers, and fifteen were short answers rating how each person felt about prayer in the schools. Following are the questions and compilation of answers.

C. The Questionnaire (Short Answers)

1. Does the person being surveyed know the Lord and Savior Jesus Christ? Explain.
2. Would the person being surveyed like prayer to be placed back in the school systems?

3. Should schools take a step of faith and put prayer back into schools?
4. Should people's constitutional rights include prayer?
5. Were schools better off once prayer had been removed?
6. Since God was banned from public schools, why have so many people wanted him back?
7. Where should Christians draw the line about prayer in public schools?
8. How could Christians change negative views about prayer in schools?
9. How would Christians raise a nation of praying children without the *breathed word*?

D. The Survey

1. Should Christians motivate teachers to become involved?
2. Should school systems allow prayer in schools?
3. Should teaching about God be put back into our school system?
4. Should the Bible be offered as an elective in high schools?
5. Should schools emphasize the Ten Commandments?
6. Should schools educate children about having Jesus Christ first in their lives?
7. Should religion be an option for the children?
8. Are schools better off today without prayer?
9. Were schools better off when prayer was a major part of the curriculum and in some cases the only curriculum?

Due to the state of the nation today, nine colleagues stated that that prayer was a necessity, that the nation was better off when the schools included prayer, and they felt that the courts should allow each school district to decide whether prayer should be included in the schools. Six people said that prayer should not be included, and four were undecided. There were only nineteen responses out of thirty-five surveys.

TOTAL RESPONSES OUT OF 35 WERE 19

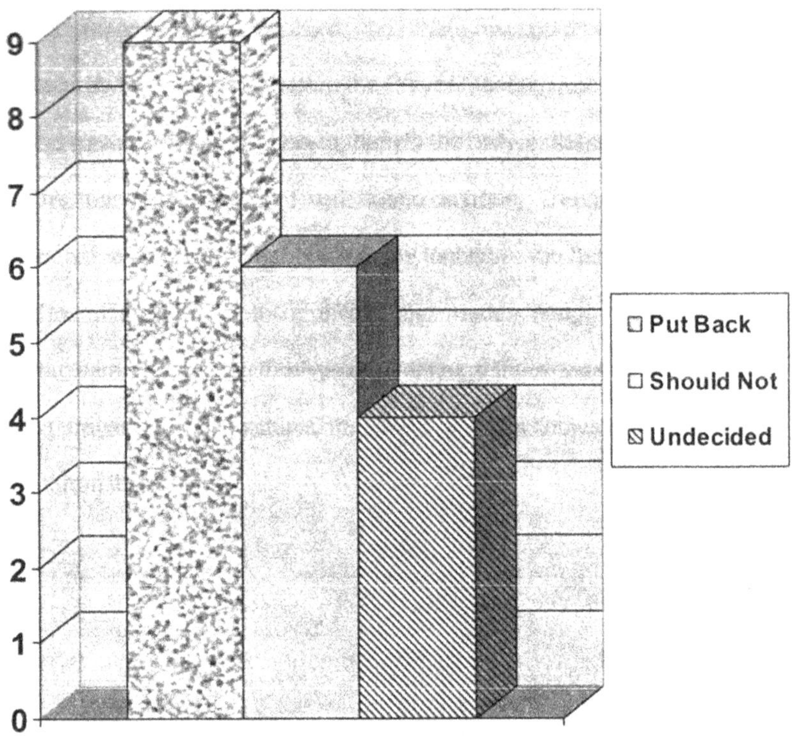

E. Conclusion

Where Should Christians Draw the Line?

The teacher knew that forming this group could jeopardize her job. However, she felt that it was time to tear down the walls and make a stand against Satan to glorify God. Though there were many staff members that refused to acknowledge God as Lord, and others that could care less, they would always stop by her classroom before the prayer meeting, just to ask the prayer warriors to include someone close to them in the prayer that day.

This teacher knew a lot of work had to be done. The questionnaire indicated that even though there were many teachers who believed in God, they were in fear of losing their jobs or of what their friends thought. Then there were those who were just waiting to be asked. Although there were still many barriers to putting prayer back into schools, the prayer warriors knew that it could not be removed from their hearts.

Chapter I
Taming Your Tongue

A. Introduction

The writer had made a decision to allow God to use her as a vessel to speak to lost souls so that God would be glorified. In order for this to happen, the writer understood that there were times when women of the twenty-first century should tame their tongue. The writer felt led to speak to women of the twentyfirst century about some of the hardships that women of the Bible had to endure. After doing tedious researches, the writer gave pointers to women of the twenty-first century so that they would not make the same mistakes as women of the Bible. The first thing that would always get in the way was women not knowing when to speak. This of course was a problem for some women of the Bible but more so for women of the twenty-first century. One example of course was women feeling a need to lie rather than be truthful in pursuit of their destiny.

B. Lying

Words were the vehicle through which women of the twenty-first century should communicate their thoughts; the tongue was the driver. It had taken many women to their destiny.[1] Women's actions and what they said should always have been based upon the

---

[1] Deborah Pegues, *Taming Your Tongue: What You Say* (OR: Harvest House Publishers, 2005), 11.

truth. Lying was like a man who built his house on the sand. This led to a shaky foundation.

Lying came in four forms: deceitfulness, half-truths, exaggerations, and flattery, according to Pegues. God had no tolerance for liars.[2] Women of the Bible explained to women of the twenty-first century how God felt about lying.

C. Deceitfulness

Deceitfulness was defined as the quality of being deceptive; falseness, concealment, and just a downright lie. Many times women of the twenty-first century found themselves in that sort of situation. Their pride had gotten in the way of their being truthful. The Lord detested lying lips, but he delighted in men who were truthful[3] (Prov. 12:22).

One of the questions women of the twenty-first century had often asked themselves was, "Why did so many people feel that they had to lie and practice deception?" Many women may have done this for financial gain whereas other women did this for social advantage, for hidden immoral acts, or for the benefits.

D. Trickster

Jacob, whose name meant "trickster," conspired concerning his birthright blessing that belonged to his brother Esau (Gen. 27). When Esau discovered the deception, he threatened to kill him. Engaging in deception was a slap in God's face, and this would have dreadful consequences. When women of the Bible had taken on a battle that was not theirs, they had taken it upon themselves to decide that God was a liar, and that he had reneged on his promise to meet one's every need. When women of the twenty-first century walked in integrity, they told the whole truth and not just part of it. Women of the twenty-first century should not rationalize a portion of a statement to cover up the truth of the matter. When women of the Bible aban-

---

2 Ibid., 11.

3 Ibid., 11.

doned that wicked behavior, God blessed them beyond their wildest imagination as he blessed Jacob.

E. Exaggeration

Exaggeration was when people embellished a story in order to get more attention from a person.[4] Many women of the Bible and *women of the twenty-first century* assumed that it was all right to exaggerate; however, it should have been seen as another form of lying. This person lost his/her credibility because he exaggerated. God had sealed the destiny of every liar.[5]

> But the cowardly, the unbelieving, the vile, the murderers, the sexually immoral, those who practice magic arts, the idols, and all the liars, their place will be in the fiery lake of burning sulfur. Their part in the lake with fire and brimstone, which was the second death.[6]

Eternal separation was too high a price for anyone to pay for any form of deceitfulness. Women of the Bible would tell the Christian women of the twenty-first century that they should continue to implore God to keep them out of that pit of deceitfulness.

F. Flattering Tongue

Both groups of women flattered others to get favors in return. Flatterers often have had a low self-esteem and believed others will like them if they complimented them. Engaging in flattery according to Pegues was clear evidence of women of the twenty-first century's lack of faith in God's ability to have given favor with other people. Favor should have been an unmerited benefit when a per-

[4] Pegues, 13
[5] Ibid., 16
[6] Revelation 21:8 (NIV).

son had appeared in the right standing with the Creator. Even when women of the twenty-first century felt overlooked, unappreciated, unattractive, or when there were other negative emotions that Satan brought their way, women of the twenty-first century should have continued to allow their mouth to speak what was true. All the words of my mouth are just; none of them is crooked or perverse.[7]

G. Conclusion

When women came to Christ, he had taken away one set of burdens—the burden of sin, the burden of exaggeration, and the burden of flattery. God called women to follow him, to have renounced their selfish desires, and to have seeded his will above all else. This cost the women of the twenty-first century absolutely nothing. Yet, those women had fallen into Satan's trap. God was not absent; he was still on the throne, working to bring about his divine purpose.

This was one of the reasons women of the twenty-first century paired up and separately took on many spiritual acts, after realizing who God really was.

[7] Proverbs 8:7–8, (NIV).

Chapter 2
Knowing God

A. Introduction

Because of biblical teaching of God's sovereignty, women of the twenty first century should believe that God possess all power on Earth and in heaven. God was the Alpha and Omega. God was where everything else rest.

Everything except God was a creation of God. God was the beginning and the end. Women of the Bible would say that women of the twenty-first century should know that the sovereignty of God stated that God should have been the primary source, the molder, love, comfort, peace, and hope. Women of the Bible would say that God was sovereign and that no king or lord had a heaven or hell in which to put God.

To say that God was sovereign would say that he was the only one in authority who decided what would be best for all things and he did this for his own pleasure. God should be supreme. None could compare. He created the entire universe. Women of the twenty-first century should have declared that he was almighty and that he was all-powerful in heaven and on Earth, so that none could have defeated him or have resisted his will. Women of the twentyfirst century should have known God as the governor among the nations, as King and as Lord.[8] God was everything. Women of the Bible have found it hard to stomach how women of the twenty-first century

[8] Arthur Pink, *The Sovereignty of God* (Ml: Baker Books, 1984), 19.

seemed to forget that God was ruler, power, and dominion over everything.[9] If women of the Bible were still alive today, they would have believed that women of the twenty-first century had a hard time getting to know the doctrine. Women of the twenty-first century should have known the basic truth—that God was the Creator and that he was sovereign. Unfortunately, for women of the twenty-first century, materialism played an important role in women of the twenty-first century's lives. On many occasions, women placed God on the back burner.

B. Know the Doctrine

To declare that the creator's plan had been frustrated by sin would dethrone God. Paul claimed that every part and that every word of the scripture was breathed by God. It was profitable first for doctrine with meaning and then for the regulation of one's daily walk. Biblical women revealed that the doctrine could not bring one correction or reproof if women of the twenty-first century did not know it.[10] The first thing profitable for doctrine through the Word of God was the doctrine itself. Everything women of the twenty-first century received must travel through a filter.[11] If women did not know the doctrine, it could not bring them conviction. There should have been some form of instructions and discipline. Women of the Bible would point out to the women of the twenty-first century that this is why God gave his breathed word, the Scripture.

C. The Scripture

The Scripture had been given by God. It was very useful for teaching, delivering, cleaning out, disciplining, and educating everyone in righteousness. It enabled Christian women of the twenty-first century to be equipped to do God's will. Doctrine meant teaching.

---

[9] Ephesians 1:21 (NIV).
[10] Pink, 213.
[11] Ibid., p. 213.

Women of the Bible informed women of the twenty-first century that all scripture was beneficial first for "doctrine," because it was inspired by God. Christian women had given heed to the first and second order. Grace and growth ceased without doctrine. The doctrine attributed to God the Father, the Son, and the Holy Spirit. Doctrine should have been an important set of guidelines to why a person believed what he/she believed. The value of the doctrine was where everything else rested.

Women of the Bible would say that the doctrine should have been the basic foundation. It was by doctrine (through the power of the Spirit) that believers were nourished and edified and where the doctrine was neglected. Doctrine was the proof of God and the connection with God, Christ, Spirit, salvation, grace, and glory. Women of the Bible would say Christians cannot separate belief and practice. Doctrine granted Christian women of the twentyfirst century divine truth and enabled them Christian character, which was that of cause and effect. This was what freed women of the twenty-first century from evil. Human will should have been the sovereignty of the servant. The will could not be sovereign because it influenced something.[12] That was why it was important that women of the twenty-first century saw God as the Alpha and the Omega.

D. Alpha and Omega

Biblical women would say that God should be seen as all-powerful. Gods regulated the affairs. He remained faithful, for he cannot disown himself. God should have been noted as holy. He could not lie (would not) because it went against his character of faithfulness. Scripture told its readers that God cannot lie and that he cannot be tempted, but was; he nevertheless could not do that which was evil.[13] God did not lie.[14]

---

[12] Pink; 50, 83, 130.

[13] Pink, 148.

[14] Titus 1:2 (NIV).

Pink stated that it must have been God's will from all eternity that all were not saved. The divine bid was that some were lost because they refused to believe. This was from the human side. The others had eternal life (were saved because they believed).

Faith was God's gift, and unfortunately all men did not have faith. Therefore, the elect were the ones that God had shown favor. Only those women of the twenty-first century that believed were ordained to eternal life. God did not bestow that gift upon all. Women of the Bible informed Christian women of the twenty-first century that they could not receive him unless they had been born again. Unfortunately, there were women that did not have the faith; therefore, they had not experienced God's favor.

No man came to the God except through the father who sent him. God spread his saving favor to the elect. Women of the Bible would warn women of the twenty-first century that the divine side of God would not be robbed of his glory. Then the women of the Bible would have a need to explain the Trinity: God the Father, God the Son, and God the Holy Spirit.

E. Trinity

Women of the Bible would then explain the Trinity. First of all, the new birth Trinity was due to the will of the Holy Spirit. God the Father, God the Son, God the Holy Ghost. Women of the Bible would go on to explain the roles of the Trinity: the Father = creation, the Son = redemption, the Holy Spirit = the work of sanctification. The Trinity represented a biblical concept that revealed the likeness of God.

With the Father, it was predestined. Women of the Bible would point out that everything was determined before people were born. The Son died for everyone so that everyone would have an everlasting life. There was none comparable to that ultimate price that God's Son paid for women, to save them from their sins, and then that Holy Spirit that revived and refreshed women so that they were born again as new creatures in Christ.

God cared about women of the Bible and women of the twenty-first century because this was just the way God was. The Son shed his blood for all, and then the Spirit did what it did (worked) in them. Biblical women would explain that what the Father and the Son did was external and what the Spirit did was internal. Because of the Spirit on the inside, women of the twenty-first century were concerned about their walk and their talk with God.

The new birth was said to have been a resurrection purposed by God. In other words it was the Father's plan from the beginning. It was the Son who made it possible when he sacrificed his life (new birth), but the Spirit who affected ones new birth. This Holy Spirit was important in order for the completeness of the Father's eternal purpose. God the Father was the origin of the Son and the Holy Spirit. Whatever the Son had received from the Father, the Spirit also had, including his very being. Women did not have the power to grant salvation. The Father, the Son, and the Holy Spirit did. The Holy Spirit overcame the native hostility and animosity of one's mind against God. Now women of the Bible felt that women of the twenty-first century should have seen God at work firsthand their lives.[15] Women of the twenty-first century all played different roles. Each part was necessary in order to have brought women of the twenty-first century salvation. Jesus said, "If anyone would come after me he must deny himself and take up his cross daily and follow me."[16] In order for women to take up their cross daily and follow Christ, women of the twentyfirst century realized that they must know the basic truth.

F. Basic Truth

Women of the twenty-first century should learn this basic truth, that the Creator is absolute sovereign, executing his own will, performing his own pleasure, and considering naught but his own glory. The Lord hath made all things for himself. To murmur against him was rank rebellion. God was in charge, doing what he wanted, as he wanted, and what he pleased so that he would be glorified. Women of the Bible would imply that it was part of God's engineered plan.

---

[15] Pink; 19, 72, 84.

[16] Luke 9:23 (NIV).

G. His Plan

Pink stated, "God governed inanimate matter, the children of men, and angels, both good and evil, and irrational creatures." In other words, God was omnipotent. Nothing in this world would have existed unless it was his plan/purpose (otherwise than God has eternally purposed).[17]

God created the earth, the heavens, darkness, light, waters, sky, dry land, vegetation, sea and land creatures, and then man out of his own image. It was all good. What Pink was saying was that everything, inanimate matter, irrational creatures, children of men, and both good and evil angels, were all created by God. He was the Creator and engineer of everything; nothing would have existed without God.

H. The Engineer

God hardened the heart of Pharaoh to fulfill his divine purpose/plan for Israel. Pharaoh tried to put God in a box as many others us do. Women revealed God's goodness only when it benefited them. God, by right of his creation, had a relationship with every human being. Through creation women belonged to God. Women of the Bible would tell women of the twenty-first century that God had engineered and sold things to the order of his will. White's five comments on Exodus 9:15, 16 indicated that Pharaoh did not get away with anything.

1. God stopped Pharaoh right in his tracks, amidst his wickedness. He was saying that God could have chosen sickness or infirmities, but instead, God cut him off by a high hand of judgment.
2. White made the statement that it was clear that God made Pharaoh and others well aware that he raised Pharaoh to punish him. That even before Pharaoh was born through infancy and childhood, in raising him to the throne of Egypt, God had a plan. God's plan was formed before Pharaoh was even born.

[17] Pink, 35–40.

3. Egypt's king had nothing on God. Instead Egypt's king was already doomed for destruction. There was none other than God that could control or tell Pharaoh what to do.
4. God hardened Pharaoh's heart just as he had promised. Scripture confirmed this. The Lord controlled the king's heart just as he controlled the wind. God used his power, and he had the right to turn Pharaoh's heart as ever he pleased. He chose to tum Pharaoh's heart against all good.
5. Finally, in Exodus 9:15–16, God revealed to Pharaoh his purpose, and in verse 27 of the same chapter, Pharaoh admitted to sinning. Pharaoh immediately stated that he and his people were sinning after he found out that God raised him up to punish him.

Keep in mind that Pharaoh also realized that it was the Lord who was righteous. The people would say God is still on the throne. The Israelites had been under the bondage of Egypt's ruler, Pharaoh. God stepped in and delivered them from bondage. In Exodus people had seen the redemption by the blood of the sacrificial lamb and the power of God. Women of the Bible would say to women of the twenty-first century, "Quit your murmuring. God does as he pleases."

I. God Did as He Pleases

Women of the Bible would share with the women of the twenty-first century that Pharaoh illustrated the doctrine of reprobation. God did not take away anyone's hope of salvation. God was the potter. As the potter was sovereign in forming vessels, God was sovereign in forming moral agents. God did what he wanted, when he wanted to, and as he pleased. God displayed sovereignty. It was safe to say that God depraved those that he did not predestine to be conformed to the image of his Son.

In Romans, Paul ultimately based God's rejection on unbelief. Women of the Bible wanted the women of the twenty-first century to acknowledge that someone may have objected to God hardening Pharaoh and not the others.

Again, God did as he pleased. Just who were they to question God? This was sin in itself. Paul was not saying that one could not question God, but that people should have been mindful of whom they were speaking. Paul was speaking to those who were speaking to God in a defying attitude, in an attempt to make God answerable to them so that they could slander his character.

God was the reason for women of the twenty-first century's total being.

God the potter made everyone. God had the freedom when dealing with women of the twenty-first century to make his power known so that he would be glorified and his plan would be accomplished. God could have chosen not to have mercy on women of the twenty-first century, yet he granted them an unmerited mercy. For example, God told Pharaoh about his purpose. He revealed to Pharaoh why he raised him. Immediately, Pharaoh admitted that he had sinned. Biblical women would say that women of the twenty-first century should keep in mind that change of heart did not just happen automatically. It was when Pharaoh was aware that God was going to punish him after he had hardened his heart and judgment was at hand, which Pharaoh tried to turn the table. Remember, Pharaoh tried. It did not happen! This was why women of the Bible felt that women of the twenty-first century should know that some people had no desire to be like God and that God does not punish the innocent.

J. Doctrine of Reprobation

Women of the Bible would speak to women of the twenty-first century about the doctrine of reprobation.

1. First, the doctrine of reprobation did not mean that God had taken innocent people and made them evil and then pronounced them as bad and worthless or as failures. Women of the twenty-first century should not charge God with the sin of his creatures. God did not take away anyone's hope of salvation.
2. Second, the doctrine of reprobation did not mean that God denied the people who were sincerely seeking salva-

tion. Some people had no desire to be like him nor did they possess a Christlike character. God was not going to force anyone to come to him.

3. Third, the decree of reprobation did not clash with God's goodness. That just because the non-elect were not part of God's favor (goodness plan) they were not totally excluded from participation in it. The unsaved had the right to enjoy God's goodness in the same way and in some cases they got to enjoy it even *more* so.

It was impossible for women of the twenty-first century to decide who among them on earth were the elect, so they did not have a right to judge any man, no matter how many times he had fallen short. Christian women of the twenty-first century should spend time cleaning their own lives according to Pink. However, this should be done God's way.

K. God's Way

A.W. Pink stated that it was because of God's kindness people undeserved favor, and God's forgiving love that people should have been born again. People did not have anything to do with it. It was all a gift given to people from God. Biblical women wanted to remind women of the twenty-first century that no human could have taken credit for their salvation. None were worthy to receive the gift of salvation, yet since God was a God of second chances and a forgiving God, there existed hope. Christian women should have had faith (believe) and hope. Women of the twenty-first century did not have the power to bring salvation. God had his way. God was the pilot. It was by grace that the unsaved had been saved.[18] This is why women of the Bible told the women of the twenty-first century that they should proclaim God.

[18] Ephesians 2:8 (NIV).

L. Proclaiming God

Women of the Bible would then tell women of the twenty-first century that they should proclaim God. Paul connected the trinity of faith, hope, and love. He stated that he was thankful because at first he was clothed in sin, away from God and they were their own worst enemy.

Biblical women spoke to women of the twenty-first century about how God rejoiced in his suffering. Paul continued to study the Word to increase his walk on a daily basis for the sake of the body (church), and he served as God had commissioned so that he would continue to deliver the Word of God in its fullness (holding nothing back). It had been God's will to make known among the Gentiles the mystery which was Christ sealed within them the hope of glory.

The church was under attack, and God had driven out all of the fullness of the Godhead. This was the gospel, and this message was for everything that had breath under the heaven. Paul reminded everyone that he had become a servant of God.

M. Conclusion

To say that women of the twenty-first century were creations of God implied that their existence had a purpose. To speak of a creation was to speak of its creator at the same time. From a teacher's perspective, if women of the twenty-first century reflected back to the book of Genesis, how God created man out of his own image, they would then attest to the fact that God created them as well.

God created people so they would see how important he was to them. He did it to glorify himself. The creation represented an image of God. He did it because he wanted the women of the twenty-first century to have the evidence of God's plan seated right in front of them. Because there as a wealth of false doctrine available, many women of the twenty-first century sometimes experienced doubt; however, women of the Bible would encourage them to proclaim God by getting to know the doctrine of reprobation.

Chapter 3
Evangelism and Discipleship Leads to Church Growth

A. Introduction

Women of the Bible would inform the women of the twenty-first century that although they prioritized their time, women of the Bible as well as women of the twenty-first century should use everyday situations as opportunities to make disciples. Having a vision and obeying the Great Commission made a difference in spreading the Gospel. It had been part of God's plan, in order to work all along. Rendering a passion for lost souls, sharing the good news of salvation, evangelizing the world, and discipling others so that they would come to know him were strategies women of the Bible used as well as women of the twenty-first century. That could move a spiritually dead believer to a mature believer in Christ. This chapter had God's purpose in mind and it listed several approaches that women of the twenty-first century should possess when considering God's plan to save lost souls. This explains God's purpose and what women of today could do to encourage positive evangelism and discipleship.

B. God's Purpose

Those who approached God's plan to make disciples must have allowed wisdom to have been their guide, as they built on the foundation laid by Jesus Christ.[19] Disciples needed to be encouraging and willing to ask God for direction.

God had a plan already in place. Christian women of the twenty-first century should be willing to serve just as Jesus served. His disciples lead the lost to him as they recruited them to a vision (God's purpose).

C. Direction

Jesus gave his disciples certain tasks and he expected them to carry them out. Because of his predestination, he knew that sometimes they would fail. Rather than criticize them, he stepped in to help. Jesus told his disciples that those that did not believe will be condemned.[20]

D. Discipleship

When evangelizing and disciplining the lost, a wise coach knew when to allow persons to make their decisions, even though the outcome may not have been as they may have expected.

Jesus had no limitations. He had a positive relationship with his disciples. The wonderful thing about this was that they knew without a doubt that Jesus loved them. When discipling others, Christians should not sit back and allow those they disciple err in belief. When something like this happened, it encouraged sin. This also prevented the sinner from developing a Christlike character.

E. Sharing Christ with Others Is Sharing Good News

The questions were, "How did evangelism, discipleship, and church growth in their community relate, and were they all necessary?" There should have been no limits when discipling, just as Jesus did not limit them! The main business (God's business) was the saving of souls! First of all, they should share the *good news with bold-*

---

[19] 1 Corinthians 3:10 (NIV).

[20] Mark 16:15–20, (NIV).

ness and confidence. This immediately *allured* people that they knew what they were speaking about and to whom they are speaking. They should have had a desire to tell people about God. It was important that people knew that they cared and that through it all, their lost souls would be saved. This immediately got their attention!

Witnessing about Christ is what evangelizing was all about. While evangelizing got a person's attention, discipleship moved a believer from being spiritually dead in Christ to becoming a mature believer in Christ. This was when church growth came into play. Sharing Christ with others was essential to a church's growth. A "healthy" church should provide its members with both discipleship training and evangelism.

Disciples should have been willing to go out into the world to *witness and serve.*

Pastor Erdie Hutchings's vision was that she, along with the leaders of her church, would show the nonbelievers how to apply the Bible to their everyday lives.

Many Americans were living from paycheck to paycheck. These people were worried about how they were going to pay their bills each month. This was probably one of the reasons pastors and church leaders often receive resistance and frustration from their members in their giving. Offering a "Get Out of Debt" workshop and having the saints apply the skills being taught reduced some of the frustrations, as they afforded the saints and community a way to take control of their finances. This type of evangelizing definitely reached the community. It taught and trained the people how to manage their income.

When people knew that this workshop was biblically based, and that it was done in a practical way, the saints suddenly became interested. Financial *peace* helped the church as well as other churches' growth. Members got more out of the workshop, and at the same time the workshop introduced Christ to them through financial principles.

F. Vision

Pastor Jerome Barber, the pastor of Six Mount Zion Baptist Temple (SMZBT), had offered this program for several years. The

SunTrust Bank sent an accountant and other representatives for a week to share with the congregation how to make wise choices, invest, become a homeowners, and how to pay off credit card debt, just to name a few. The church was congested with members and nonmembers. Many church members admitted to not tithing due to other financial priorities. This workshop taught members how to take control of their finances. Money was an issue that affected everyone inside and outside of the church. Pastor Hutchings's vision was to teach couples how to work with money.

Pastor Barber introduced this workshop years ago. In the last ten years his church has grown from three hundred to five thousand plus members. His members had continued reaping the rewards.

Brian D. McLaren (*More Ready Than You Realize*) spoke about street evangelism. He stated that some people on the street saw it as a way of selling God, while others saw it as a way of shoving one's personal ideas down others throat. Television, according to McLaren, meant to some "rehearsed sales pitches and was non genuine tears!"[21]

G. Evangelism

Pastor Hutchings and McLaren both agreed that evangelism was an essential need that the world factor most. According to an unknown author, "People did not care how much one knew, until they knew how much one cared!" McLaren stated that good evangelists were those who offered hope, showed kindness, had taken something ugly and turned it into something beautiful, were truthful, had values, had a purpose, had meaning, and talked to others about faith. This was the goal of the women.

In order to be an effective evangelist, Christians should have had a *Christlike* character. Good evangelism was being friendly without being prejudice according to McLaren. It was having a positive impact on others while it led people to Christ. McLaren explained evangelism quite well when he claimed it to be the "style of Jesus."

---

[21] Brian D. McLaren, *More Ready Than You Realize* (Grand Rapids: Zondervan, 2002), 14–15.

Once people had begun to feel evangelism and live it, they had greater desire to help others to do the same. According to McLaren, because of its amazement, they wanted to share it, and anyone who heeded the messages should dance. McLaren said that when they evangelized, anyone who heard the word of God, truly heard it, could not sit still. They were to dance! This was all part of a cycle. One lost soul learned about salvation, heard it, applied it, and then he shared it with another lost soul. They were inspired about this awesome God, who awaited them. They continued to spread the word to other lost souls.

McLaren spoke of all the people who wanted some answers to their spiritual questions. He stated that they were more ready than they realized throughout his book.

Members in Pastor Hutchings's church told her that they had considered her their mentor. She witnessed to them in the wee hours of the night. This had been tiresome. However, Christ's door was always open. How would she try to be like him if she was not willing to make the sacrifice?

H. Judging Them

It was so important that people knew that they were not judging them. Some people were a little reluctant at first because of their lack of trust. One of the first things Pastor Hutchings told them was that "*God loves them.*"[22] She told them that in spite of whatever they had done, God loved them and so did she. She tried to relate whatever the situation they were going through to scripture in the Bible. Many times she found them apologizing or they stated that they did not want to be a burden. She had to stay in control, be patient, gentle, and know that giving of one's self was part of being a disciple.

[22] John 3:16 (NIV).

Pastor Jerome Barber, senior pastor of Sixth Mount Zion Baptist Temple, was asked to speak on the mission of his church. His response:

> The five elements I am about to address represent the mission statement of Sixth Mount Zion Baptist Temple. When I became pastor of this church ten years ago, I wanted to develop a way to keep the church focused on what God had called us to do. These actually six elements have evolved over the ten years of my pastorate.
>
> 1. Exalting Jesus Christ. God made us for worship and God made us to worship. We believe that deserves our worship. We intentionally create an atmosphere that encourages people to worship. Psalms 100 says enter his gates with thanksgiving and enter his courts with praise. Let everything that hath breath praise the Lord.
> 2. Edify the body of Christ. The word *edify* means to build up. Our aim is to create an atmosphere that encourages the members of the body of Christ to be strong in the Lord.
> 3. Evangelize the world. The great commission given by Christ has not changed. We are challenged to go into the entire world preaching the Gospel and making disciples.
> 4. Extend the love of Christ. Jesus said that we are identified as his disciples by how we love one another. The true demonstration of the depth of our commitment to Christ is seen in how we love and treat one another.
> 5. Excellence in ministry and in service. All the service we provide should be done in a spirit of excellence because it is being done as unto

> the Lord. There is an additional element that represents the totality of our mission statement. The sixth element is critical in the fulfillment of what we do; it is equipping the saints to do the work of the ministry. The Bible says in Ephesians the fourth chapter that the way the church grows strong is that each part does its part. The strength of a strong church is determined by the strength of the membership. If the Lord shall tarry, I pray that Sixth Mount Zion Baptist Temple will continue to be a church that is making a positive difference in the lives of people.[23] Jesus became so successful. The word says Jesus grew in wisdom, stature, and favor with God and man. As we intentionally approach ministry, I believe that we will continue to create disciples of Christ. We will continue to grow in our faith toward God, and will have such a strong faith that it will not fail us as we face challenges in life. We will maintain healthy relationships based upon the scriptures.[24]

The Bible instructed his members to go out into the world and share the Gospel to all nations. Pastor Hutchings believed that evangelizing the world was not an option but rather a requirement, or a command from the Father. Saving a soul was one of the most important things a disciple had done. It was crucial that this task had not been taken lightly. There were various groups of people, e.g., the backslider, the new believer, the nonbeliever, and based on how

---

[23] Luke 2:52 (Pastor Barber's interview continued). (Permission to include in paper).

[24] Statement by Doctor Jerome Barber, personal interview, Dec. 21, 2007 (not edited by author).

a certain group of people that may have received the message, each person should be approached differently.

It was crucial to have had a certain strategy when evangelizing others, particularly those who did not have a personal relationship with the Father. It may have been even harder for those who actually received the Gospel! So how did they approach this? The most important factor, of course, should have been that of *prayer.* The Bible stated that receiving the word of the Lord was something that was "spiritually discerned." If a man's heart has not been prepared by the Father and the ground was not solid, his message had not been received. There was also a slight chance that that person would be annoyed.

Evangelists should have been sensitive to that matter. As Christians, they should not have wanted to take the risk of making nonbelievers feel that they were being forceful and judgmental. Secondly, the greatest gift that a disciple should offer was the word. Having lived by the principles and lived by the standards of the Gospel not only showed the Lord that they loved him, but it sent the message God's people were *serious* about their faith and that they were not hypocrites. Nonetheless, the Lord rewarded those who faithfully stayed in his face. When the nonbeliever actually saw the results of Christians living a fruitful life, this served as a motivational tool for sinners to accept Christ as their Lord and Savior.

In essence, the best thing a church should do was first and foremost to prepare a group of strong, serious, believers, who were able spiritually to discern the Lord's commands, to approach those whose hearts and minds had been prepared to receive the *good news.* The church should use all of its resources (e.g., television, radio, traveling, volunteering, and just being a good brother or sister in Christ) in order to spread this good news.

Reaching the youth in the church was another way of reaching other youth when spreading the Gospel.

An eighteen-year-old youth responded to the question, "Did evangelizing others influence sinners to come to Christ?" He stated, "Absolutely!"[25]

---

[25] Statement by Brandon Hutchings, personal interview, December 24, 2007.

I. Stay Involved

Pastor Hutchings's vision was to invest her time, come to serve, and not to be served. This was often said by Pastor Barber. He demonstrated this on a regular basis. One example was when he cooked dinner for the leaders of the church or when he had taken his last dime and gave it to the less fortunate. This was an example of what motivated others to become disciples. The vision God had given people in his divine plan was to build an intentional ministry of disciplining teenagers.

Jesus used spontaneous occasions to disciple people. To the twelve disciples, God gave them Jesus. Jesus spoke about his mission. God gave these men his Son, with two purposes in mind, that they should be with him and that he might send them forth.

Pastor Hutchings's vision was that her church would offer crowd, group, and individual discipling. One of the things that had led to the growth in her church was the developing commitment in disciples. Christ was first in her life, and this commitment expressed itself in the way she served, visited the sick, led Bible study classes, and participated in other ministries.

As a pastor, she tried to stay involved in what the members had done, showed an interest in her church family, as well as the community, and she had a servant's heart. She met them on their turf as Jesus did when he visited in Peter's home, when his mother-in-law was ill. It showed that she cared enough about them to enter their (non-Christians') world and that she was willing to get involved in their day-to-day struggles, regardless of the obstacles.

If they get involved in a more spiritual friendship, if they identify evangelism as a dance, step-by-step process, rather than an event, and learning experience for all parties uninvolved, rather than a sales pitch that others view, what it means to be a Christian will change.[26]

God's plan was that his disciples blessed the world, not just the church.[27] The only way this would have been done was to have had

---

[26] McLaren, 171

[27] McLaren, 187.

a vision of changing the world. People should know what God's plan was and then to have acted accordingly, with his grace. When they spoke of making disciples of all nations, this meant that they must have loved and have respected everyone regardless of their ethnicity. God loved them, and they were all his children. Therefore, the ones God loved should love one another with *agape* love. So many times Christians tended to impose their values on other cultures. They should have been assisting in drawing souls closer to Christ, yet because of their selfish intentions, they allowed self to get in the way and, in some cases, they glorified themselves.

J. According to Webber

According to Webber, there were three important insights for evangelism:

- Evangelism requires many steps (procedures).
- Evangelism did not just happen. It had taken time. People had to go through the process.
- Evangelism brought new converts to spiritual maturity as they continued to grow.[28]

The *Great Commission* was not only to evangelize but to make disciples of all nations, so the lost would come to know Jesus.

According to Webber, the early church taught three principles for evangelism:

- Be open, not biased.
- Live it, teach it, preach it, and enact and live an extraordinary Christian life.
- Create a community that cares for the needs of the world.[29]

---

[28] Robert E. Webber, *Ancient Future Evangelism* (MI: Baker Books Company Inc., 2003), 13.

[29] Webber, 57.

K. Networking Is a Part of Church Growth

Webber spoke about how the church had been a hospitable community of people who worked through different "social networking."[30] Social networking was a way of contributing to a church's growth. Visitors and nonaffiliated persons that traveled from church to church—converts, disciples, and new members—could all add to a church's growth.

Webber indicated that churches should provide a convert with a rite of passage. It was like a guide that enabled the persons to mark a spiritual journey. He also stated that evangelism and discipleship must have been understood in the Christian culture.[31] He implied that churches needed to get involved with more than just their church and community. He urged Christians to minister to the world without being biased and prejudice. Although they evangelized in a new work, the message was still the same. It was the culture that changes; God never changes. The drawback was many Christians did not have a clue to how they should communicate this message in the Christian world. Webber encouraged them to return to the ancient process.[32]

William Hutchings Jr., Pastor Hutchings's son, a juvenile probation officer in FL, was asked to describe what he would like to have seen in a disciple.

Reach out to them with welcoming arms and a warm spirit. Be fishers of men (Scripture used by evangelists). Be responsible for them. Let others know that there is a way to God through Christ. Let them know that you will be supportive. Help them transition. Don't use big words. Communicate on their level. Let them know that you too have sinned. Be sincere! Share your experiences that lead you to Christ. Relate experiences with scriptures. Let them know that God loves them in spite of, and that he will always love them.[33]

---

30 Webber, 57.

31 Webber, 134.

32 Webber, 134.

33 Statement by William Hutchings Jr., personal interview, December 25, 2007 (permission to quote William Hutchings).

Brandon Hutchings, another son of Pastor Hutchings, a student at Bethune-Cookman University, explained how his life changed when he needed a breakthrough.

Every day I think about a word and somewhat dwell on it. Today I came across the word *success*. To most, this word simply means a good finish or a good result, but to me it means a little more than just that. Success to me is the conquering of one's fears and the achieving of God's plan. I believe that if it can be thought of or revealed, then it can be done. Under my standards, it is pure happiness after an accomplishment that was worked through with an enormous amount of effort, with God's help. Struggle and achievement falls under that category as well. I feel that it is common knowledge that God's will is going to be accomplished with or without you.

Over the last couple of months, I have experienced success in many different ways, or you could just say areas of my life. On November 17, 2007, I decided to practice and practice until I knew I had reached the level of an all-district band player. On December 10, 2005, I was informed that I had made the all-district band. My decisions to practice led me to a successful outcome. On December 12, 2005, I decided to become part of the media ministry at my church. My decision led me to an internship with Motorola. Again, that was a huge decision, which led to a huge success. There was no way that any of this could have been accomplished without God. Because of an evangelist taking the time to talk to me about salvation and his taking the time to show me how to have trust in God, I made it.[34]

Success could have been described in many different ways. The fact of the matter was that it was a complete process of plans, aspirations, decisionmaking, overcoming setbacks, and possibly, even failures. Nothing was possible without God. "If they were to think it, then they could have dreamed it; if one had dreamed it, then they could have achieved it" (author unknown). However, all the glory belongs to God! Therefore, both evangelism and discipleship played an important role in winning lost souls, witnessing about Christ, and increasing church growth. It was an intricate part in winning lost souls.

---

[34] Statement by Brandon Hutchings, personal interview, December 25, 2007.

Yalonda Hutchings, Pastor Hutchings's daughter, a medical doctor graduate student at Duke University, was asked to define the word *disciple.*

I believe there is a disciple of men, and that there is a disciple of God. In *Webster's Dictionary*, it states a disciple is one who embraces and assists in spreading the teaching of God. In the Bible, it says a disciple is one of the followers of Jesus, who adhered to his teaching and transmitted it to others. A disciple can be categorized as a leader. One must lead his people to success before he can be successful. To be a true disciple, one must take up his cross daily and follow God (sic).[35]

Chrystal Daniels, daughter-in-law of Pastor Hutchings, an elementary teacher in West Palm Beach, FL, was asked how her church could promote growth.

Ways that a church can promote growth is to be more encouraging. They should offer mental health programs, financial workshops, etiquette ministries, and tutoring programs for the children. There should be a parents' night out once a week, and the church should be family oriented.[36]

The vision in Pastor Hutchings's heart for evangelism was sincere. First of all, she had a passion for God and she was commitment to teaching the Gospel. Her vision included an evangelistically training program for those who felt a call to evangelize the world. Although many obstacles got in the way, there was no stopping her. God had chosen to use her as a vessel to help lost souls come to Christ.

Apostle Paul had taken a risk to become all things to all people, for the sake of the Gospel, with the Holy Spirit.[37] God had enabled Pastor Hutchings to take some powerful risks in order to make her ministry abundantly blessed. Her plan was to employ all her gifts, talents, resources, and her members to help her make her ministry a success.

---

[35] Statement by Yalonda Hutchings, personal interview, December 29,2007 (permission to quote).

[36] Statement by Chrystal Daniels, personal interview, December 29, 2007 (permission to quote).

[37] 1 Corinthians 9:22–23 (NIV).

L. God Should Be Glorified!

Author Mark Mittelberg spoke very highly about evangelizing against the odds. Although Christians show interest in evangelizing in their culture, there was confusion about what to believe and whom to trust. Although these suspicions arise, many are willing to take that risk. Visitors attended different churches, hoping to find an answer.

Mittelberg spoke from experience when he spoke about the joy and advantages, when one tried to reach lost souls with a catchy (contagious) church.

In order to reach outsiders, Christians have unlimited vision and an inwardly and outwardly focus. People did not want to feel as though they were a burden. They needed to know that people were sincere and not acting for personal gain. Churches needed to come together, collaborate, and then be supportive of one another in order to build contagious churches with unlimited results. Many churches were content with their number of members and budget. They had forgotten about God's purpose for which the churches were founded. Mittelberg stated that church should have become a contagious place that won more and more lost souls. If this was the case, why did this not happen?

After attending several churches, interviewing several Christians, and doing a little research, Pastor Hutchings found that each church focused on its strongest area. Apparently, each church had its plan, but that was unnecessary. God had a plan!

Churches tended to have stated their mission in ways that were more suited for their congregation. In order for any church to become contagious, it should have leaders that know exactly where they were going, how they were going to get there, what their goals were, and then they should have been willing to work hard and pray without ceasing to fulfill God's purpose. God has already placed the proper people and resources into place in the churches. However, when things looked hopeless, like not getting the funds to build a larger church, or the members were not active participants, pastors usually looked for an easy way out. In some cases, they created a plan. What this did was display their lack of faith.

Before doing anything in this life, people should pray. Why? Satan of course! Satan would rather have kept them busy than have them build contagious churches. The people that were lost were Satan's prey. Satan detested Christians! Therefore, he was willing to do *anything* to win them over. Satan knew that Christians were there to increase God's kingdom and to destroy his, so he tried to keep them distracted. He tried to destroy them.[38] People should have been very careful of Satan's tactics!

In order to build a contagious church, prayer was the key. People should have sewn it into the realms of their every being. Once this was into play, they could build successful churches where everyone would have been connected to Christ. In order to do this, biblical training was essential. When doing anything to glorify God, and it was part of his plan, the good news was that they had *his approval.*[39] However, Satan continued to be against them. This was why it important that people resist the devil.

In order for any church to become a contagious builder, a church should have offered diverse programs, music, events, and other outreach events so that outsiders would not feel misplaced.

Mittelberg spoke on two principles that applied to the task of building a contagious church. Christians must first be sure that God has called us to that mission. Second, we must also get clarity about how to carry out those tasks.[40]

Pastors needed comprehension of what was involved, then he would take some risk, working long hours, realizing that there will be some setbacks. This was when they should remind themselves that their setback opened the door to opportunities.

The question often was asked, why are they trying to do this? People matter to God! Just when they think that no one cared, someone came along and reminded them that God cared. Pastor Hutchings firmly believed that when people knew that they mattered

---

[38] Mark Mittelberg, *Building a Contagious Church* (OR: Zondervan, 2001), 27.

[39] Ibid., 27.

[40] Ibid., 34.

to God, their actions began to change. Everything they did could be affected by this.

One example was when people paid their tithes. They were blessed because they were doing what was required of them. People tended to take for granted that others knew how important they were to them. God informed his people that he loves them so much that he gave his only Son.[41] Regardless of what a person was going through, just knowing that they mattered, that someone loved them, would soften their heart.

All were lost unless they knew Christ as forgiver and leader. Zacchaeus received salvation after Jesus went into his home.[42] Jesus implied his mission was to seek and to save what was lost.[43] He was saying that one could not be saved until he was found by him with his grace. When people they had been lost, they realized it was not a pretty sight! Members should have been serious about their call to build contagious churches. If a person did not know Christ, he was headed straight for hell. Each person has sinned and fallen short of the glory of God.[44] Therefore, people needed to get to know Jesus, and they needed a personal relationship with him.

Jesus said plainly, "I am the way, the truth, and the life. No one comes to the Father except through me."[45] Peter added, "Salvation was founded in no one else, for there was no other name under heaven given to men by whom they must be saved."[46] People needed to know that there was no way they could get to the Father unless they went through Jesus. One really needed to comprehend what was being said. They needed to heed the message of the *Cross.*

It was the power of God for the salvation of everyone who believed.[47] Although sinners were sometimes challenged, they questioned why Christians were right and sinners were wrong. Non-

---

41 John 3:16 (NIV).
42 Mittelberg, 37–38.
43 Luke 19:20 (NIV).
44 Romans 3:23 (NIV).
45 John 4:6 (NIV).
46 John 4:6 (NIV).
47 Romans 1:16 (NIV).

Christians felt that Christians should respect their views and keep an open mind.

People needed to have more than just someone to proclaim the Gospel. They needed to have meaning and to have it defended.[48] They also needed to know who, what, why, when, where, and how to follow Christ.[49] Mittelberg called them roadblocks, when people had begun questioning the existence of God. In order to assist people in their move toward Christ, Christians needed to proactively address certain issues to show that their Christian faith was built on the word of God.[50] "We demolish arguments and every prevention that sets itself up against the knowledge of God, and we take captive every thought to make it obedient to Christ."[51]

Many pastors have tried to reach those that came from a broken home. These people felt isolated and alone.[52] They had experienced the pain firsthand. This was why so many people joined different cults and other world religions. Those non-Christian teachings offered them a sense of family and community, where it was lacking in their lives. The question was so often asked by pastors, "How did they draw in believers?" Where two or three came together in Jesus's name, they would be warned and drawn in, both by human relationships and divine presence.[53]

According to Mittelberg, once outsiders got a taste of what a real Christian community was like, many had an urge to respond to the Gospel, and they became members of God's family.

In order for missionaries to have successfully communicated in a foreign land, they must have studied that country's culture and language. This was the only way the missionaries would have communicated the Gospel. What many Christians failed to realize was that

48 Mittelberg, 42.

49 Mittelberg, 42.

50 Mittelberg, 43.

51 2 Corinthians 10:5 (NIV).

52 Mittelberg, 46.

53 Matthew 18:20 (NIV).

the church and community were cultures unto themselves.[54] No two people were the same, nor did they have the same values.

Mittelberg quoted Billy Graham as saying, "Instead of becoming salt and light, we have been content to withdraw into our separate ecclesiastical ghettos, preoccupied with our own internal affairs and unconcerned about the deepest needs of those around us." Mittelberg indicated that the further we go into our direction and the further the unchurched go into theirs, the harder it will be to reach the unchurched.[55]

One needed to be motivated like Paul. Paul was more than willing to accommodate himself to various cultures so that the people in that culture would come to know Christ. He was very careful about doing nothing spiritually out of bounds while he ministered to other cultures. Paul wanted them to follow his example and run in the race.[56] Being culturally relevant should not have been ignored. They needed to approach each group differently. No two groups were the same, nor had they experienced the same things. Adaptation and hard work would definitely be involved. Christians should effectively have reached into an unsaved person's world, spoke their language, illustrated the true gospel, and with the Holy Spirit, led those lost souls to Christ, as they strived to get closer to Christ his secular world where they were led by the Holy Spirit.

Most pastors were trying to reach people right away. Paul stated that they needed more time. Today, however, some people doubt the mere existence of God. They want to limit his creations and abilities. Sinners need time to let it sink in about the goodness of God. This was one reason Christians should not rush people into beliefs about spiritual truth claims. This would have been foreign to them at first; therefore, they needed a little more time to sort out the process. Christians needed to encourage and challenge the unsaved to keep praying and to continue pressing toward the mark. They should not force the lost to take that leap into their direction right away.

---

54 Mittelberg 48

55 Mittelberg 48

56 1 Corinthians 9:24 (NIV).

Christians should be willing to go everywhere, and anywhere, to proclaim the true gospel.[57]

Evangelism should be a form of discipling. Disciples are people who are content in Christ, as they work toward winning lost souls.

Every church is driven by something. This can be a strong force. However, in order for any church to be successful, it must have a purpose that pushes it forward. A church must not be unhealthy.[58]

A healthy church was one that nourished its members, fed them God's Word, equipped the saints, evangelized the world, and it had compassion, just to name a few. When a person became part of a church, it was usually because God has sent them there. That person was usually searching for something.

M. Enabling Strategies

Five strategies that could have enabled a church to grow were warm fellowship, discipleship, worship, ministry, and evangelism.[59] There should have been convictions and, of course, principles in order to have built an effective church. In order to have had a strong church that discipled, evangelized, and produced growth, it must have a plan in place. Many pastors assumed that population was what made a church successful. They assumed that as long as people continued to join that church on a regular basis, that their church would have had an effective ministry. Clubs also drew in large crowds! God made no mistakes about what his plan was and people were held accountable for not carrying it through. When God said move, move!

In order for any church to have growth, it should have sent out the right messages to the people. It should have offered people something that they could not get any place else.

Some churches allowed the needs of the unbelievers to be their main focus. When they did what they thought was right, it excluded God's purpose. According to Rick Warren, attracting unbelievers was

---

[57] Mittelberg, 59.

[58] Rick Warren, *The Purpose Driven Church* (Ml: Zondervan, 1995), 49.

[59] Ibid., 49.

okay, but this was not the only step to making disciples and evangelizing the world. It was fine to be sensitive to the needs, pain, and interest of nonbelievers; however, they could not allow seekers to alter God's plan. Just who were they trying to please?

Churches should also have refrained from just filling positions. They should be more focused on developing people. Only God's plan will last forever. Before any plan was in force, the first thing that members of a church should have known was why they existed. When churches were built for the eternal purpose of God, members had motivations, direction, foundation, unity, and God's approval.

Pastor Hutchings's perception of evangelism was spreading the good news of God's love. It was a contribution by God to his servants, to share the great news of his sovereign love, as the lost were called to repent, have a personal relationship with him, and to do as Christ had commanded them to do. They should have been more warming, welcoming, hospitable, and caring, to everyone.

When unchurched people attended Pastor Hutchings's church, they were expecting God to do something in their lives. When meeting with ministry leaders of the church, Pastor Hutchings encouraged them to see the needs of visitors to the church. The visitors saw this as a new beginning.

Visitors were used to hearing, "Will all visitors please stand, or is there something we can do for you?" What made them think that the visitors or the unchurched folks wanted to share anything about their personal life with them? Being a vessel of God and a pastor of a church, Pastor Hutchings strongly recommended that they allow the visitors to do most of the talking.

Before the disciples do anything, they should have asked them if they should pray with them about some of the needs that they were having. Prayer did not have to be elaborating. A simple lifting up of their personal needs was great. They should not make promises that they would not be able to keep.

Often people did just that. When they prayed, they should pray with compassion. People needed to know that someone cared. This showed them a little about themselves as well as their relationship with God. It also reflected their beliefs.

Let them know that though their prayer may not be answered right away, one day, joy will surely come! Share with them that although they may not have gotten the response they wanted, that God did what was best, and he made no mistakes. One should keep in mind that once the unchurched person had seen an answer to prayer in the course of time, God would use them to witness and draw that person's family closer to him. This was evangelizing, spreading the good news!

One of the things Pastor Hutchings experienced was that saints should not just leave visitors in their church hanging. After the service ended, believers should not run off. The problem with many believers was that they were in too much of a hurry. They needed to partner with each other, then and when the appropriate time came, believers should spend some time introducing visitors to members of the church. This would make visitors feel more welcome.

When they did this, it afforded the Christians the opportunity to see the guest for who they were and not for whom they would like them to become.

Christians must be willing to go beyond the call of duty and put on the Christlike character, marinated with love, compassion, and understanding. They should pray for patience. They should be available to listen to their stories, listen to their needs, and if necessary, offer them a shoulder to cry on. On many occasions, Pastor Hutchings was in a situation like this. Through it all, sinners wanted to try Jesus. Pastor Hutchings stated it was her responsibility to allow God to use her as a vessel to help introduce the unchurched to her Lord and Savior, Jesus Christ. Many Christians believed that in order to become an effective evangelist, they must be able to memorize certain verses in the Bible. Although this has always been helpful and encouraged, it was only the tip of the iceberg.

According to many modern pastors, the Gospel was extremely powerful when shared with love, clarity, and simplicity. Let the people know that God had his/her back. Let them know that Jesus wanted a trusting relationship with them. But first, they must be willing to admit that they were responsible for excluding or fighting God from their lives. This was when the pastor should ask them if they would like a relationship with the Father. Let them know that this relationship would last forever. Tell them that God cares about them, especially them.

Evangelists should serve Jesus who commissioned them to disciple the nations. Though many view scriptural authority and affirmations differently, God provided clarity! People were empowered to be obedient and embrace each other.

God wanted his followers to do everything without complaining or causing a negative disturbance.[60] This would enable them to be without blame. People were always watching. Most importantly, they could not hide from God.

They should make every effort to be without blame.[61] Therefore, they must always be reminded of the fact that he chose them before the foundation of the world.[62] If they walked in integrity, their offspring would also be fruitful and blessed.[63]

One reason some churches were not doing evangelism was because their pastors neither did evangelism nor valued it. Some would ask, "What did one have to do with the other?" Everything! God has blessed them to teach and to preach. These were all privileges. Evangelism should have been a part of a teaching and preaching process. They worked as a system.

Pastors should have a strong vision and passion to reach lost souls all over the world. People (believers and unbelievers) thirst for a deep spiritual relationship with others. If they did not find it in their church, they would find it elsewhere, usually places outside of the church. Churches that have had a desire to reach or minister to the unchurched should be willing to develop ministries that addressed this deeply felt need for fellowship.

Luke said, "The Lord added to their number daily, those who were being saved."[64] Why did one evangelize? It enabled Christians to tell the good news with the purpose of winning lost souls.

---

[60] Philippians 2:14–15 (NIV).

[61] 2 Peter 3:14 (NIV).

[62] Ephesians 1:4 (NIV).

[63] Proverbs 20:7 (NIV).

[64] Acts 2:47 (NIV).

One of the pastoral concerns was why so many churches were in decline. Many pastors were desperate for answers to why certain churches were doing better financially and spiritually. They attempted to implement whatever was happening in the successful church into their churches. Others required members to show their pay stubs. Yet, those pastors could not understand a few months later why their church was split. Members were then ready to excommunicate the pastor.

In order to build any kind of model for the church, there was a preparation process. Members were extremely demanding, and there were so many nonparticipants in the church. This too was a pastoral concern. What worked for one church may not work for the other.

One of the biggest problems in Pastor Barber's church was that they had over five thousand members with less than thirty percent tithing faithfully. This caused the faithful few to be overworked and pressured to increase their tithes. Yet, the ones that were just showing up on Sunday were the main ones complaining.

N. The Doctrine of Grace and the Sovereignty of God

The doctrine of grace and the sovereignty of God were exciting and contributing to life changes. Both of these encouraged believers to witness internationally and exalt Christ. When teaching of God's sovereignty, in sinners, salvation was God made.

When showing evangelistic passion, people should consider four truths with non-Christians.

1. God loves everyone.[65]
2. A person's sin hinders him from having God in his life.[66]
3. God's Son died so that sinners may have an everlasting life.[67]
4. Everyone could receive this eternal life by admitting to God that he is a sinner and asking Jesus to forgive him.[68]

---

[65] John 3:16 (NIV).
[66] Psalm 51:3 (NIV).
[67] 1 John 2:2 (NIV).
[68] 1 John 1:9 (NIV).

Christians did not need to rush all of this on to the non-Christians at once.

Give them time to think things through. Keep in mind, non-Christians were spiritually dead. They had no clue. Placing all of this on them at once was like teaching them a foreign language for the first time. Christians needed to keep in mind that they were still growing in Christ. They should only explain God's revealed portion of salvation!

Let the non-Christians know that they served a sovereign God. They should point out that all of this revealed knowledge that was being shared with them had come from *God.* Confess that all were once lost. Witness about how they could fall in love with Jesus.

When it came to witnessing, Christians sometimes allowed pride to get in the way. They thought that it was their responsibility to get sinners into God's Kingdom. It was not! They were only supposed to let others know about God's goodness and show them how to get to him. They were to allow God to do the rest. Many of the unchurched never attended Sunday school or church service. They had no idea about Jonah and the big fish, Daniel surviving in a lion's den, or Jesus sacrificing his life so that they might have eternal life.

Sinners had no idea what this means. Christians needed to take the time to explain salvation, sin, the blood of Jesus, and grace.

When witnessing about God, Christians needed to display God as truth, through his revealed Word, and do it with respect and love. When people did not share their past before they came to know Christ with others, they were sending off mixed messages. They were giving the sinners the impression that they had always lived a perfect life with Christ and that they were perfect.

This immediately turned off nonbelievers. How could saints lead the unchurched to Christ if they could not be honest with them? Christians should be mindful of their feelings as they listened very carefully to others. They should keep in mind that someone had to take the time to listen to them before they became a Christian. They needed to have a heart like Jesus. Jesus welcomed them with open arms, and they continue to share his goodness with the rest of the world.

O. Conclusion

When women of the twenty-first century conveyed the good news of Jesus Christ, it was good, but when they had a relationship with Jesus Christ, it was *awesome*! Women of the twenty-first century realized that when they approached and hit people with the love of Christ, it really worked. This was why it was so important that women knew that they could not witness without having church.

It was important to let the unchurched know that all have fallen, but with God's grace, they could recover. Rendering a passion for lost souls, sharing the good news of salvation, evangelizing, taking the time, and discipling, so that others may come to know him, are all parts of God's plan.

There was no need when discipling and evangelizing to make things any more complicated than they already were. It was more important to be "clear" than "clever." It should not matter why one's sisters and brothers all over the world were coming to Jesus. What mattered was that "they were coming." Women of the twenty-first century's vision was to have fewer "ought to" and more "how to" sermons. Having a revelation that was part of God's vision was stamped with God's seal of approval—a vision so well displayed by women of the Bible.

Chapter 4
Postmodern Women in the Church

A. Introduction

Postmodern is relating to art, architecture, or literature that reacts against earlier modernist principles, as by reintroducing traditional or classical elements of style or by carrying modernist styles or practices to extremes.[69] When trying to close the gap between modern and postmodern people, Christians should develop a personal, lifelong, obedient relationship. With Jesus Christ, making it evident that they had transformed their character into Christ likeness, changing his/her values into kingdom values involving the unsaved into his/her church mission, home, and the world. This could be just the right ingredients to help that lost soul.

Women of the twenty-first century tended to have had a better chance of becoming leaders today, and although they may have encountered some hardships along the way, it depended on their strengths as well as their experiences to get postmodern people to accept them.

Women of the Bible would also speak to women of the twenty-first century about postmodernism and how to communicate God's purpose. According to two Hearst tabloid journalists, women

[69] Donald Hagner, Document Page: Postmodern Philosophy, (n.p.9/30/08). http://find.Gale group.com. Postmodern Defined.

outnumbered men in the government world, and they slept their way to the top.[70] Ellen Vargus of the Legal Defense Fund argued that separate sex education for women has historically meant inferior education.[71] Critics claimed that separate classes for all males meant inferior education for women.

1. It could diminish multiculturalism. Other women argued that it was shocking that black males who once stood in solid support of ensuring equal and integrated classroom would support same-sex Sunday school classes.
2. Discriminating on the basis of gender, these groups, some argued, should be taught in the most narrowly tailored circumstances to remedy past discrimination.

B. Know Your Target

Women of the twenty-first century should communicate their purpose with excellence and define their goals. Contagious churches resulted when leaders knew what they were trying to reach, and then worked tirelessly and prayerfully to fulfill God's purpose.

God respected women of the Bible. If God favored them, who could be against them (Rom. 8:31)?

C. Components to Reach Postmodern Thinkers

In order for women of the twenty-first century to reach lost souls, they must have a plan and a purpose that should include the following components:

- Women should know how to approach the unsaved
- Women should build relationships with people outside the family of God.

---

70 Document Page: Attacking the Washington (Femmocracy): Antifeminism in the Cold War Campaign apainst "Communists in Government" (Essay) (Storms, London, p.29, n.d,). "http://gale group.com

71 Liz McCloskey, Custom Journal Document: *Boys and Girls Together*. (n.p, n.d).

- Start witnessing/tell the unsaved about how God saved them.
- Answer questions/be honest when answering questions.
- Crossing the lines of fire/do not be so eager to prove a point.
- Follow up/keep in contact with the person.
- Review and practice it/get some feedback on what drew them to Christ.
- If the church people are going to reach the culture with the church, they must understand the culture. Do research about that culture.
- Christians should work on their personal spiritual development.
- Leaders should set the P.A.C.E.
    - Prayerful and prepared/stay in the word and pray without ceasing.
    - Be accountable and available.
    - Be caring and committed.
    - Lead by example.
- Leadership is a privilege and not a right!
- What does an educator look like?
- Crowd (unsaved) Isaiah 43:18–19
- Community (unchurched)
- Congregation (Sunday only)
- Committed (disciples)
- Core (leadership)—go through crew
- Active in recruiting—engage
- Values that can influence non-Christians beliefs in some cases can have a negative effect on the unchurched when Christians try to impose their values on others. It turns them off.

D. Faith and Order in the Postmodern World

Every aspect of the title gives one pause. First faith and then order. The Faith and Order movement came into existence early in the twentieth century to address the differences over faith and order that divide the church. These divisions and the disputes were not new.

The problem that set the Faith and Order agenda predated modernity and will, short of a new outpouring of the Spirit, be around when postmodernity is a footnote in history textbooks.[72]

When women paused, they saw the need for the topic. Division over matters of faith and order predate the modern and postmodern worlds. The Bible should represent a source of historical information or of religious and moral, or theological concepts.

Postmodernity and its relation to modernity are defined. There have been cultural, intellectual, political, and economic changes in the last several decades that can be grouped together as a move into at least a new form of modernity.[73]

E. Christian Unity

The Bible offered a site of contact that signified Christian unity. Once Christians could agree on language and practices in relation to Scripture and worship, then they could become more open to diversity in a more precise conceptual languages. Postmodernity raised challenges to meaningful notions of truth. Faith and order required a firm sense of truth but must also prove sensitive to the social dynamics of truth. This claims truth could relate to the assertion of power. Could pre-modern texts (which were questioned in the modern era) be at home in the postmodern world? Could ancient scriptures still speak in the postmodern world? In other words, would the postmodern world accommodate the Bible? Many people laid the blame on the unchurched people whenever ideas and behaviors made them nervous about postmodern cultures. Many have defied postmodernity because they felt that it did not exhibit and sustain faith or have respect for order. Christians did not feel comfortable in the postmodern world because it appeared inconsistent. It challenged religious and cultural traditions.

---

[72] Postmodern Philosophy, 9/30/08.

[73] Document Page: *Postmodern Defined* (n.a., n.p., n.d.).

F. Postmodernity

Postmodernity appeared as a current that pulled swimmers away from shallow shores. A rip current forms when waves break unevenly; usually the ends break first, then the waves fold inward and gush back out to sea at the middle, creating a ripping pull that is much stronger than the power of the waves that came from the deep. The rip current became scary for swimmers who tried to swim against it, for it is like swimming upstream against the strong white waters of a narrow but deep river; it can be deadly (those swimmers can drown).[74]

Postmodernity tended to confuse Christian educators, shake the foundations of order, and disturb structures of life's purpose. This perception could possibly misguide the unsteady and the doubters. To reach postmodern thinkers, Christians should enter their world and assume their identity. Upon understanding their culture and values, one realized that this invited weaving with their beliefs. Christians should remember that he/she should adapt to other cultures when teaching. Postmodern people should have a sense of security.

Women educators should affirm that the Bible represented all Christians. Christian women must see their teaching ground. They were considered great for some, but they were considered not great for everyone. Reclaiming teachings through evangelism enabled a way of communicating. Storytelling was one way of refusing to let go of biblical teachings. What was (or makes something) home for a postmodern subject?

Context conditions identity, and so does home (in the form of family, food, customs, clothes, memory, story, tradition, etc.). Context is present; home is transcendent, across "the river," over yonder. One way to make this elusive home present is through recalling memories and telling stories. The postmodern turn in literature and cultural studies is an invitation to the ruins of representation; the invitation uncovers traces of tribal survivance, trickster discourse, and the remanence of intransitive shadows.[75]

---

[74] Michael Root, Journal of Ecumenical Studies: *Faith and Order in a Postmodern World* (n.p., 2007). http//elibrary.com.

[75] Gerald Vizenor Magazine Journal: *Ruins of Representation* (n.p., n.d.) http//elibrary.com.

Unfortunately, regardless of how hard spiritual women taught, men continue to have a problem with women being their leaders in the twentyfirst century! Whereas some had this instilled in them, others blamed it on the Bible. Could it be a male ego thing, or did the Bible really prove that men are the leaders?

Erdie M. Hutchings, the teacher, was doing this questionnaire to find out why there was such a gap in women and men attending Sunday school. Included in this paper, only one man agreed to do a questionnaire.

Although several were asked, only one responded.

G. Questionnaire/All-Male Sunday School Class[76]

1. Do you have a personal relationship with our Lord and Savior Jesus Christ?
2. How long have you been attending your church?
3. What do you feel about women liberations?
4. How many books are in the Old and New Testament?
5. Can you give the Scripture that tells how the revelation (thoughts of God) was written by man?
6. Can you name five women in the Bible?
7. Can you name at least five women listed in the Bible that were allowed to take own leadership roles, as appointed by Jesus?
8. Are you married?

Read 1 Timothy second chapter, verses 7 to 22 then answer the following questions:

1. How did Paul say men ought to pray?
2. What did Paul caution men about?
3. Did women teach in the early church?
4. Where was Timothy serving when he received a letter from Paul?

---

[76] Erdie Hutchings, teacher, composed the questions.

5. Who was Timothy's mother?
6. Can you define divine?
7. Can you define sovereign?
8. Why did Paul send a letter to Timothy?
9. How do you feel about all-male Sunday school class?

One of the challenges postmodern cultures of the twenty-first century tend to focus on was the issues that many men had about women teachers and leaders. While a particular person who attended an all-male class had no problem with answering most of the questions in the questionnaire, it became a challenge when asked why he attended an all-male class. After a short hesitation, he stated that he had no problem as long as the person taught God's Word without being biased. However, he stated that based on First Timothy, second chapter, verses eleven through fourteen, he could see why there would be so much confusion about women teachers.

In his interview he stated that Paul was ordained (appointed a preacher, and an apostle), so he knew what he had to speak about concerning women as teachers. He firmly believed that Paul found fault in women speaking in tongues publicly, so this is why he had some doubt about women teaching men, period.

He felt that since men should be over women in spiritual matters, this proved an incentive for men to be the spiritual leaders.

Paul did not say that women could not be spiritual leaders. He tried to encourage men to take on spiritual leadership roles. In this postmodern world, women had been faced with so many women spiritual leaders because men would not step up to the plate. The questionnaire had not been a challenge for the men at first; however, when asked about women being spiritual leaders, they became a little reluctant to continue the interview.

On the internet a viewer found it more amusing to focus on Sarah Palin's attire when he should have focused on her plan for the nation.

In what flesh should a preacher dress the Gospel for God to reveal himself to a postmodern audience, bring about their conversion, and enfold them into his family?[77]

Sarah Palin, former mayor of Wasilla, Alaska, age forty-four, attended several evangelical Christian churches according to the *Los Angeles Times*.[78] An unusual video showed Palin, the Republican vice president nominee in 2008, being blessed by a Kenyan bishop against witchcraft, which brought many concerns among liberal bloggers and angered others. However, some religious leaders stated that it had been blown out of proportion by ignorance and intolerance. Would all of this publicity have come about if this were a man? Just how much of it comes from women haters? Does being a woman give others the right to degrade her spiritual beliefs?

This witchcraft line immediately brought attention to liberals. Keith Olbermann, host of MSNBC's *Countdown*, called the video terrifying and said it made the Rev. Jeremiah Wright, the much-criticized ex-pastor of Barrack Obama, look quite mainstreamed in comparison.

One of the viewers in the article said these words: "I don't know why they are making a big thing out of it." Olupana said of the media reaction to the video, "Witchcraft as part of a belief system is real to the people who live there," he said, noting as there was "nothing unusual about what happened."[79]

There were reasons to question the choice of the commander of Alaska National Guard as a prospective commander in chief just as there were equally serious reasons to doubt the military qualifications of another backwoods candidate.

Women of the twenty-first century could question first, what did this rhetoric concern have to do with Sarah Palin's qualifications to be president? The idea of a divine image found in every human should prove that the main foundations for his/her American tradition of liberty, tolerance, and pluralism. Religious responsibilities

---

[77] http: www.politico.com/news/stories/0908/14102.html (n.a., n.p., 2008)

[78] http:www.news/stories (n.a., n.p., 2008).

[79] http:www.polilico.com/news/stories/0908/14102.html (n.a, n.p., n.d.).

should motivate millions to love and serve their neighbors as women respect their rights of conscience. This video would deride Palin's religion and produced a bunch of bitter and angry folks.

This working mother of five, who was down-to-earth, electrified the Republican Party. This US presidency reflected a new attitude toward women in a political standing. Polls suggested that Governor Palin's role as Sen. John McCain's running mate for the November 4, 2008 election against Democrats Barrack Obama and Joe Biden had definitely enhanced the Republican ticket with female voters.

News reporters should not focus so much on the person delivering the message. They should focus on God's Word that had been instilled in Jesus. They should also do as Paul had instructed: to speak spiritual truths with his/her heart and his/her mind. This would definitely allow them to focus more on God's word rather than on the gender of the teacher.

Author Alan Nelson, who wrote a book, wrote a typical Sunday message that has the best chances of connecting, will have approximately three to seven info chunks.[80]

In other words, women of the twenty-first century should have a purpose, provide concreteness and vividness, to connect in more memorable ways.[81]

Men and women should arrive at an answer. However, because men think differently, they may not arrive at an answer the same way as do women. Therefore, both men and women should translate principles in terms of concrete relationships, while caring enough to speak their language.[82]

H. Postmodernism

Postmodernism reveals a desire to understand the present culture. There tends to be a growing ignorance of the Bible not only

80 Alan Nelson, *Creating Messages That Connect: 10 Secrets of Effective Communications* (CO: Group Publishing Inc. 2004), 64.

81 Ibid., 6–129.

82 Chris Altrock, *Preaching to the Pluralists: How to Proclaim Christ in a Postmodern Age* (MO: Chalice Press, 2004), 45.

in society in general but also in the church. The authority of the Bible may be said to be in shambles. The interpretation of the Bible appeared increasingly in jeopardy. All of this has made it more and more difficult for the church to hear the Bible as truly the Word of God. However, the Bible was God's gift to the church, one of the most important—indeed, indispensable—resources. Christians should do all they could to bring it back to the church. This could be done by strengthening one's commitment to the importance of sound exegesis. They must hear the Word of God and then help all of God's people hear that Word, for the world. God remained the only sure anchor among the confusing voices of this lost world.

I. State of the Bible

Every generation, it seems, has worried about the state of the Bible and has addressed the issue of the apparent ineffectiveness of the Bible in the church. As a sampling, I mention the following publications. In 1969 the Netherlands Reformed Church produced a volume titled *The Bible Speaks Again* (Minneapolis: Augsburg) designed to bridge the gap that has developed continuously during the last hundred years between the biblical scholars and the man in the pew.[83]

It appeared that people of today trusted the Bible less than in the past days. The authority of the Bible suffered over the last century. For most people, the Bible represented basically a good book. As with many other good books, its readers had to pick and choose what they liked from its contents. In short, the Bible appeared to be heard for what it was, the written word of God. It seemed to be no longer the book of books, but a book among many books. Many store it around for a kind of protection, security, and good luck!

The reasons for this erosion of authority are not difficult to discern. We live in an increasingly secular world where science seems to have trumped the Bible. Gospel of Judas—matters that constantly

[83] Jione Havea, Magazine Journal Document: *Ecumenical Studies* (p. 547, 2007). http//find.galegroup.com.

catch the attention of the media—people are led to believe that the Bible does not tell the truth, or at least not the whole truth. What the Christian church has believed for two millennia now turns out, it is alleged, to be but one stream of late thinking that became dominant through a power play that designated and oppressed earlier Christianities as heresy. There remains the widespread, lingering suspicion that real scholarship has debunked the Bible.[84]

People are trying to put religion with politics. It appeared difficult if not impossible to speak of truth. A key difficulty also arose from within, namely, the abuse of the Bible by (mainly) conservative Christians. There seemed to be a gap between the best scholarship and popular conservative Bible reading. A variety of clergy appeared on TV stations and regularly showed little ability to do better with the Bible. There were many other issues, a number of them very controversial, such as the place of women in the church and the unqualified support of Israel.

J. The Historical Method

What should women of the twenty-first century do with the fact that the historical method had been so destructive of the Bible? Viewers needed to focus more on the Word rather than the speaker wearing a dress.

Postmodernism challenges the entire edifice of modernism. It rightly indicates, first, that there is no possibility of complete objectivity or neutrality in our quest for knowledge. We all bring our own biased perspectives and presuppositions to the task of knowing, whether we are aware of it or not. Second, all of our knowledge is necessarily fragmentary and short of absolute. All human knowledge is therefore necessarily partial and imperfect. So far so good, we may say. But when these insights are pushed to their extreme, they can lead to the impossibility of knowledge altogether, to agnosticism and even nihilism. The very idea of truth must be dismissed; all that is available to us is opinion, and yours is as good as mine.[85]

---

[84] Magazine Journal Document: http://find.galegroup.com, 2007.

[85] Postmodern Philosophy, (n.a., n.p., 9/30/08).

Women and other theologians have had a huge impact upon the interpretation of Scripture. Meaning lay in the reader and not in the text. It seemed a little like contemplating women's ideas. The Bible had evidently lost its authority in the twenty-first century. An analysis of the method led to the reactive emphases of postmodernism.

Some educators believed that young people could learn more in singlegender schools than in coeducational institutions, but in instances where such schools had been established, legal challenges has forced them to open to both genders.

While the compression of the world through current systems of economics, migration, media, and technology could make twenty-first century Christians acutely aware of globality, the movement of persons and ideas through global systems was not unique to biblical time. The conviction of medieval theologians that no spiritual women lacking Christian faith and baptism could be saved had been conditioned by the fact that their world became practically co-extensive with Christian Europe. Given the limits of their horizon, it proved understandable that they could have presumed that people who were not Christians had heard enough about the faith to be guilty of having rejected it.

Spiritual women should look at the state of the Bible in the twenty-first century, focusing on its loss of authority because of the influence of a particular kind of historical criticism and because of the rise of postmodernism. Christian women must insist on the importance of exegesis, especially for those who aspired to take the Bible seriously, which in turn would cause them to take up some loose ends from his/her discussion of postmodernism. Women should look at some practical suggestions for the church in light of the content of two lectures together. Once this idea surfaced, women could boldly take on many leadership roles.

Nothing had been as heartwarming in the field of biblical studies over the past few years as the new emphasis on the theological interpretation of Scripture. Theological interpretation brought readers' aims into play in the process of interpretation. The primary aim of the believing reader was to hear the voice of God in the Scriptures, and not merely to hear but to hear responsively, in a transforming way, and in a way that issued forth in obedience. Theological interpretation desired to approach Scripture on its own terms, that is, in keeping with its own intentions.

The responsible use of Scripture could help restore appreciation for the authority of the Bible. Women of the twenty-first century should avoid the idea that nobody could really interpret the Bible correctly and that they could prove anything from the Bible! Christians needed to prioritize it, increase the number of required courses in exegesis, and make an effort to stress it throughout the curriculum and not just in biblical courses. They should have a responsible biblical interpretation in every course in order to get postmodern people to listen.

The area that many Christians felt guilty could be their failure was the area of spiritual formation. The worship services of the local church should be that the majority of Christians encounter the word and the sacraments. Although Christians must encourage church members to become daily Bible readers, even Bible students, for many the hour and a half in church on Sunday mornings could remain the only input from the Bible they received in a week. This time should be maximized. In this secular world, Christians were bombarded with a steady stream of the world's distorted values and perspectives. It would prove hardly possible to counteract this with one and a half hours per week, but Christian women could not afford to squander the time they had available. Like most people in this society, whether or not they would express themselves this way, they were hungry for God's Word. The thriving success of what had been called generic spirituality proved evidence of this hunger.

Christianity had so much to offer people of which they were quite unaware. It should be up to Christians to make it known. Many congregations had this exactly backward. They apparently thought that the pastor should do all of the work of the ministry. How sad, and how common too to see the pastor bogged down with running the church: administration of every kind, calendar, programs, personnel, and the budget. Meanwhile, the flock had not been fed adequately. Sermon preparation had to be squeezed in where possible, and pastors certainly could not take the time that a fresh exegetically based sermon would require. If they were to preach effectively, pastors needed to have budgeted as sacred time a good number of hours per week for the study of Scripture and for sermon preparation. If pastors could correct only this problem, the situation of the church would be greatly improved, and there probably would be more Christians and more male leaders in the church.

A growing ignorance of the Bible existed not only in society in general but also in the church. The authority of the Bible could be said to be in shambles.

The interpretation of the Bible in the churches was increasingly irresponsible. This contributed to the warning authority of the Bible in the twenty-first century.

It should go without saying—but it is important nevertheless to make it clear—that there is much that is good about postmodernism and even much that can be used in support of Christian faith. Let us begin with its justified critique of modernism. As the product of enlightenment euphoria, modernism embodied an overconfident belief in the ability of autonomous human reason to know everything and to know it absolutely.[86]

Postmodern women should have had the opportunity to share freely rather than having to stick legalistically to a plan developed for the postmodern thinkers. Women teachers should have shared experiences that related to the content being taught. They should have allowed God to work while enabling postmodern people to respond during a teacher setting. When trying to get postmodern people to except God in their lives, Christian women leaders should have become human models and provide positive instruction and accountability, so they one could have become what Christ had intended them to become. NonChristians would see the spiritual leader as someone who had followed Christ long enough to lead by example rather than seeing that they are women.

Leading by example could have a more positive effect, model the behavior, and offer hope to the unsaved. Once he/she has reflected

[86] Postmodern Philosophy (n.a., n.p., 9/30/08).

on these concepts, it could have been just what the unsaved person needed in order to give his life to Christ.

Postmodern thinkers should be taught how to pray, as they seek God's direction. Women teachers should use everyday situations as opportunities to encourage the unsaved to give their lives to Christ. A positive thing when getting the unsaved to turn their lives over to Christ would be to teach the unsaved how to have a relationship with Christ. The postmodern people often gave their lives to Christ when they faced a crisis. This was when he or she became the most teachable. Christians must keep in mind that no one way of winning souls worked with everyone. Postmodern people could become true Christians if they felt loved, and Christians respected their culture. They must have felt a sense of trust and love. Many postmodern people responded to the love. The unsaved had shown them.

Postmodern women must also have something in their lives that the unsaved needed. Postmodern people would welcome women spiritual leaders once they witness firsthand the qualities they wanted in them that they did not have. Christians must be totally committed to Christ. They should be someone that had it all together—a whole, well-adjusted person with strength of character. In order for spiritual women leaders to get the attention of postmodern people to really listen, they must have possessed an effective ministry and proved willing to show others how they could have the same. These women leaders must have possessed a good home life and integrated their spiritual and secular lives.

Postmodern people should be recruited to a vision rather than a program or organization. This could take them from one point to another. Positive women leaders should share the vision God had given them in his divine plan.

Christians should offer them the opportunity to share what God had done in their lives.

Christians should also show an interest in others. This communicated a servant heart. Postmodern people would be willing to listen if Christians meet them on their terms as Jesus did when he visited Peter's home when his mother-in-law had become ill (Mark 1:29–31). Doing this could demonstrate commitment. It would show that they cared enough about the nonbelievers to enter their worlds and get themselves involved in their day to day struggles. Meeting them outside of their comfort zone took special effort signaling that they cared. The heart of effectively drawing postmodern people to Christ would be living Christ's commands and then teaching them. Spiritual women should not ask others to do something unless the spiritual women are willing to do it themselves. By this, women should practice what they preach.

Women of the twenty-first century should be willing to provide guidance until the unsaved person became more skillful and comfortable with one's new life. This would enable the postmodern people to apply what they had learned while at the same time, the new converts would be getting support as they began to live their new lifestyles.

K. Conclusion

Looking at what the Apostle Paul had to say about women helped women of the twenty-first century to figure out how they should approach postmodern thinkers. Although women of the Bible had taken on several lead roles, women of the twenty-first century were afforded more opportunities in the modern world. What women of the Bible needed to get women of the twenty-first century and postmodern women to do was to bait the hook and heed the following:

1. Have a purpose.
2. Adapt to the other culture.
3. Know the teaching ground.
4. Teach the text.
5. Show caring.
6. Have a vision.
7. Provide guidance to postmodern people.

Women of the twenty-first century should guide these lost souls, have compassion, and share past experiences.

Chapter 5
Women of the Bible Spoke to Women of the Twenty-First Century

A. Introduction

Women of the twenty-first century have come to realize their difference from the women of the Bible. Did these women have something so significant to tell? Of course, after meandering through the Bible, they found that certain attributes of human nature remained the same over time. Embracing the gifts from the ancient women in the Bible enabled women of the twenty-first century to find some insight into wisdom![87]

Women of the Bible suggest that women of the twenty-first century should remain obedient to God's word, and they should concentrate on how to please God rather than on issues of the past that women of the Bible had to endure. Women of the Bible were saying that women of the twenty-first century should learn from their mistakes of the past so that history did not repeat itself. Women of the Bible were also saying that women of the twenty-first century had been blessed with resources to help carry out a plan that had been predestined by God.

---

[87] Vanessa L. Ochs, PhD, *Sarah Laughed* (USA: Library of Congress, 2005), 228.

B. Subordinate Figures

Although Bible women for the most part were shadowy, subordinate figures, particularly in the Old Testament, there were those like Eve, Delilah, and Jezebel who stood out, each with a distinction of her own. Whether queens or commoners, virtuous, chaste, or bad, their lives proved the Bible a faithful biography of human nature.

While the ancient world seemed predominantly a man's world, women enjoyed a high status in Israel.

C. Old Testament Times

Israelite laws protected women's weaknesses, safeguarded their rights, and preserved their freedom.[88] Under divine law, their liberties were greater, their tasks more varied and important, and their social standing more respectful and commanding. The Bible acknowledged women with wisdom, skill, and dignity. "If his master gives him a wife and she bears him sons or daughters, the woman and her children shall belong to her master and only the man shall go free."[89] While the husband had no formal rights over his wife, he seemed recognized as lord and master.

> She watches over the affairs of her household and does not eat the bread of idleness. Her children arise and call her blessed; her husband also, and he praises her: "Many women do noble things, but you surpass them all."[90]

Women of today could have earned a lot of respect because of their love and diligence within their family and their community.

---

[88] Deuteronomy 21:10–14; 22:13; 22:28; (NIV).

[89] Exodus 21:4 (NIV).

[90] Proverbs 31:27–29 (NIV).

D. Early Church Times

When a Samaritan woman came to draw water, Jesus said to her, "Will you give me drink?" The Samaritan woman said to him, "You are a Jew and I am a Samaritan woman. How can you ask me for a drink?"[91]

Through the examples of Jesus in his attitude toward women, and as the result of the truth he taught, women have increased in prominence.[92] "If he comes alone, he is to go free alone; but if he has a wife when he comes, she is to go with him."[93] The apostles placed high standards for Christian women and exalted women as a type of the church, the Lamb's bride.[94] Women ministered unto the apostles from their substance and came to hold official positions of spiritual influence in the church.[95]

E. Present Times

Through the centuries the social and legal status of women fluctuated. In times of fierce persecution they suffered. Women in the United States of America later experienced universal education after the Nineteenth Amendment, which granted women the right to vote. Through the impact of the Christian faith, they became equal with men in the achievements of education, art, literature, and social services. Woman of the twenty-first century seemed to chase sin, exalt divorce, and pervert sex, all springing from a rejection of Christ godly women appeared noble and beneficial for their homes, nation, and church. God-inspired women showed devotion to the homes, their husbands and children, and the Bible.

---

[91] John 4:7, 9 NIV.

[92] John 4:7 (NIV).

[93] Exodus 21:3 (NIV).

[94] 1 Timothy 3:11; Titus 2:3–5; 1 Peter 3:16 (NIV).

[95] Romans 16:1 (NIV).

F. Marriage

"Haven't you read," he replied, "that at the beginning the Creator made them male and female, and said, for this reason a man will leave his father and mother and be united to his wife and the two will become one flesh."[96]

Jesus emphasized the indissoluble nature of marriage.[97] Originally, God sanctioned monogamy, that is, the marriage of one wife or husband at a time.[98] From the earliest days in ancient Israel, marriage symbolized festive joy, whether secular or spiritual, as well as the union and communion between God and his people. God blessed them and said to them, "Be fruitful and increase in number; fill the earth and subdue it."[99] God created Adam and Eve, made of one flesh, to populate world.[100]

G. Family

The Bible mentioned many mothers. The constant reference to them in the biographies of successive kings indicated their importance as determining factors in the lives of their royal sons. Among the Jews, women administered the affairs of the home with liberty. Women were in no sense the slaves of their husbands. God's law required children to honor the mother equally with the father.[101] God promised a prosperous life.[102] Judgment overtook those who cursed their parents.

The Bible said God created Adam and Eve in his own image.[103] The first chapter of Genesis led to the climax of creation. God formed

---

[96] Matthew 1 9:4, 5 (NIV).

[97] Matthew 1 9:4 (NIV).

[98] Genesis 2:24–25 (NIV).

[99] Genesis 1:28 (NIV).

[100] Genesis 1:28 (NIV).

[101] Exodus 20:12 (NIV).

[102] Psalm 127:4, 5; 144:12–15 (NIV).

[103] Genesis 1:27 (NIV).

Adam from dust and then breathed life into him.[104] Genesis chapters one and two recorded the creation of the universe, which included the solar system, plants, fowl, other animals, and humans. While man did not have all the details of how all things came into existence, the Bible confirmed that God created them.

Genesis chapter three told the story of Adam and Eve's disobedience to God's law.[105]

H. Eve

Mikil Raver, in his 1998 book, *Women of the Hebrew Bible*, stated, "Eve succumbed to the wiles of Satan and the steps leading to her surrender are illuminating—she saw, she coveted, she took, etc. 'The tree was good for food'—bodily appetite was tempted. It was 'a delight to the eyes'—her sensuous nature was tempted. Then, 'the tree was to be desired to make one wise'—the most powerful temptation of all, namely, 'the spiritual temptation to transcend the normal experience of men and to taste of the wisdom that belongs only to God.'"[106]

Eve was responsible for the fall of man. She shared the fruit with Adam.

Because Eve listened to the snake and ate the fruit of the forbidden tree of knowledge, pain and suffering came.[107]

Eve's rebellion was the first biblical clue that the Creator gave humans a free will. Risking immediate death, Eve ate from the tree. Eve had a choice: stay safe and obey God, or disobey and gain increased knowledge. God set forth one rule for Adam and Eve. "And the Lord God commanded the man, you are free to eat from any tree in the garden; but you must not eat from the tree of knowledge of good and evil, for when you eat of it you will surely die."

Painfully will you get your food from it, all the days of your life. It will yield you brambles and thistles, as you eat the plants of

---

[104] Genesis 2:7 (NIV).

[105] Genesis 3:17 (NIV).

[106] Miki Raver, *Women of the Hebrew Bible* (CA: First Chronicle Books, 2005).

[107] Genesis 3:16 (NIV).

the field. By the sweat of your face will you get your food, until you return to the earth, for from it you were taken. For dust you are, and to dust you shall return.[108]

According to Virginia Owens (*Daughter of Eve*), in the book *Women of the Hebrew Bible*, with the possible exception of Mary, Eve seemed the most misunderstood woman in the Bible.[109]

Name Meaning—there were three names applied to Adam's wife:

1. Woman
2. Man
3. Adam

Eve was referred to as a woman, because she came from a man.[110] Both Eve and her husband were called Adam. Male and female created he them…and called their name Adam.[111] God made them one flesh and gave them one name. Eve, the name given her after the transgression and its prophesied results, seemed the choice of Adam who called his wife's name Eve, because she became the mother of all living.[112] This name described her function and destiny in spiritual history of which she became the beginning.

The product of a divine creation, Eve appeared as a complete, perfect woman. She never experienced being a child, or a daughter, or a maiden. She came out of Adam. Eve's daughter was the first female born into the world.[113] Having existed in God's thought, Eve appeared upon the earth. God created Adam out of the dust of the earth, but God created Eve out of a bone taken from Adam's side. Eve became the first wife. God witnessed Adam's innocence, so he did not want Adam to be alone. It would benefit spiritually, intellectually, and socially for Adam to marry. Adam needed someone to

---

[108] Genesis 3:17 (NIV).

[109] Virginia Owens, *Daughter of Eve* (CO: Zondervan Publishing House, 1995), 13.

[110] Genesis 5:2 (NIV).

[111] Genesis 2:23 (NIV).

[112] Genesis 3:16, 20 (NIV).

[113] Genesis 5:4 (NIV).

love and bear his children to complete the command "to multiply and replenish the earth."[114]

Eve had no inherited sin. Coming from the hand of God, Eve had an advantage no other woman knew. She appeared pure and holy with the divine image unimpaired. Created sinless, she became the world's first sinner, and introduced sin to her offspring. Everyone after her became "born in sin and shaped in iniquity."[115] Eve, fresh from the hand of God with unmatchable grace and beauty of body and mind, sinned. Ruin followed and paradise surrendered.

Eve was the first woman Satan assailed on Earth. When God created Eve, she knew no wrong. Satan insinuated in the cleverest way to Eve that there was nothing to worry about in eating forbidden fruit.

What about her husband? Adam did not restrain Eve from eating the fruit.

Pain and suffering followed.

Eve became the first mother to have a son who became a murderer.

Sorrow and anguish followed her transgression! When Cain, her firstborn, came into her life, Eve loved him. She named him Cain, meaning "to get" or to "possess" or "acquisition." Her second son was named Abel, a name implying "that which ascends" or "a vapor"—something doomed to fade. Eve became the first sinner and Cain became the first murderer.

Through Eve's sin, death entered the world, but at the cross Jesus conquered sin and death.[116]

The world's first woman, first wife, first sinner, and first mourner, Eve learned two lessons from her sin. Eve's story had proven women's inferior reasoning and their intrinsic feminine deceit. Women's independence came to an end when Eve chose to imitate Adam's response to the divine interrogation.

---

[114] Genesis 1:28 (NIV).

[115] Romans 7:21 (NIV).

[116] Genesis 3:13 (NIV).

Biblical women learned how much of a catastrophe Eve and Adam caused, not just for the human race but for God; he must have suffered when he sent those original children forth to make their way in the world.

I. Delilah

Delilah, a woman who used her personal charm to lure a man to his spiritual and physical destruction, stood out as one of the lowest, meanest women of the Bible.

The Bible gave no knowledge of her parentage and background other than to say she came from the valley of Sorek, which extended from near Jerusalem to the Mediterranean.[117]

After Delilah had put Samson to sleep, she called a man to shave off the seven braids of his hair. The Philistines captured Samson, gouged out his eyes, and took him to Gaza! They placed him in prison to rot.

Delilah said to Samson, "Please tell me what makes you so strong and what it would take to bind and subdue you." Samson answered, "If I were bound with seven fresh bowstrings, which had not been dried, I would become as weak as an ordinary man."

So the Philistine chief brought her seven fresh, strong tendons, still moist. She bound him with them. Now she had men concealed in her room, and she called out, "Samson, the Philistines are upon you!" He broke the tendons as easily as a string snaps at the touch of a flame. The secret of his strength remained unknown.[118]

Samson revealed the secret of the Nazirite strength to the seducing Delilah, which immediately brought shame to himself.

Delilah seemed devilish; she had personal charm, mental ability, self-command, and nerve, but used all her qualities for one purpose—money.

Womanly honor and love had never met, for behind her beautiful face was a heart as dark as hell. Deluding Samson into believing

---

[117] Judges 16:4 (NIV).

[118] Raver, 100.

she really loved him, Delilah sold him to blindness, bondage, and death. The ease with which she betrayed her husband revealed that she belonged to the enemies of God's and Samson's people, the people of whom Samson became a recognized leader at that time.

Samson became a traitor to himself because he fell for a woman's charm. First one woman and then another took advantage of his deep-seated weakness, and Delilah was the most effective in destroying him. She remained as a warning to all men, beware of the charm and wiles of a wicked, scheming woman.

Judas later sold Jesus for only thirty pieces of silver. Delilah shared her tempter's passion for revenge. She set about in a subtle way to earn the price of blood. She tried four times in her cunning, evil way to get Samson to reveal the secret of his supernatural power. A weeping woman melted his heart, and he confessed the truth of his Nazirite vow. He became like any other man. After Delilah recognized the truth, she lulled Samson to sleep. As he slept, the waiting Philistines destroyed the sign of the vow, and when Samson awakened, although he tried to exert his power as before, he found it had deserted him.

Cutting his hair degraded the spiritual Hercules. Samson knew that his bitter servitude was a result of his sin. But out of the depths of despair, Samson cried unto the Lord, and his hair began to grow. Though people lost respect for Samson, God restored the power Samson had lost. Samson's weakness became God's strength.

What lessons could God's people learn from Samson and Delilah? How could future generations learn any lesson from such an unpleasant story?

Feminine charm and the appeal of love were gifts received from the Creator. However, when Delilah misused these gifts, divine retribution came into existence.

Another lesson from the ancient record would be the unequally yoked. Samson married outside his own country, people, and religion. Had Samson, hero of Israel, married an Israelite maiden, the tragedy that had overtaken him would never have happened. He married against the divine decree, and he paid the fatal price for his action.

J. Jezebel

Name Meaning—Jezebel, the woman known as a she-devil. This heartless woman with a bloody history belied the name she bore, for Jezebel means "chaste, free from carnal connection"; but by nature she seemed a most licentious woman. No name became more inappropriate for such a despised female. We could say she was so evil that the meaning of the name changed, and future generations thought of evil when they heard the name Jezebel.

K. Family Connection

She was the daughter of Ethbaal, king of the Zidonians, and both king and priest of Baal worshippers. The Phoenicians were a remarkable race and outstanding maritime people of the ancient world, but they were idolaters who regarded Jehovah as only a local deity, "the god of the land." Jezebel sprang from an idolatrous stock, the same source that afterward produced the greatest soldier of antiquity.

Jezebel was a Phoenician princess who came to Israel through an arranged marriage. Her parents were the king and queen of Sidon, as well as high priest and priestess of the religion of the goddess Asherah and of Asherah's consort Baal. Both Jezebel's foreign origins and her faith were strikes against her. Not only did Jezebel embrace paganism, she encouraged her husband, King Ahab, to do the same.

Savage and relentless, this proud and strong-minded woman carried out her foul schemes. A gifted woman, she prostituted all her gifts for the furtherance of evil, and her misdirected talents became a curse. Persuasive, her influence was wrongly directed. Resolute above other women, she used her strength of character to destroy a king and her own offspring, as well as pollute the life of a nation.[119] Jezebel was a formidable woman, clearly much stronger than her Israelite husband. That was another strike against her.[120]

---

[119] Herbert Lockyer, *Their Finest Hour* (USA: Fleming H. Reveal, Publishing Co., 1979), 74.

[120] Raver, 136.

It may be that Ahab was more luxury-loving and sensual than cruel, but under the complete domination of a ruthless woman, he was forced to act against his finer feelings. Jezebel was rotten root and branch, and thus everything connected with her was contaminated.[121]

Elijah was a zealous prophet intent on uprooting pagan worship and determined to crush Jezebel. In *Biblical Literacy*, Rabbi Joseph Telushkin writes, "It comes as a shock to turn to the biblical texts in which Elijah appears, only to learn that the traditional kindly and lovable prophet bears no relationship to the Elijah of flesh and blood. The most furious and confrontational of the prophets, Elijah may well be the Bible's angriest figure."[122]

Their gods were Baal and Ash Toroth. Jezebel, the heathen woman who married Ahab, king of Northern Israel, and who in so doing became guilty of a rash and impious act, which resulted in evil consequences. Ahab, captivated by Jezebel, "took her to wife, and went and served Baal and worshipped him." All the other sins of Ahab were light compared to his marriage with Jezebel and the serving of Baal that followed.[123]

She possessed an extraordinary force of character. Jezebel appeared no ordinary woman. Her demeanor attracted immediate attention.

She seemed a dominating wife. Ahab seemed as a puppet in the hands of his overpowering wife. Due to his weakness, Jezebel found it easy to achieve her murderous designs. How could spineless Ahab resist the evil scheming of his unscrupulous partner? Jezebel became the feared commander in Israel.

Ahab seemed the weaker vessel with a wife who mocked at his conscientious scruples and bound him in all wickedness as with strong chains.

Her offspring continued the wickedness they lived as children. Jezebel's evil influence became revived in her daughter, Athaliah of

---

[121] Lockyer; 74, 75.

[122] Raver, 137.

[123] 1 Kings 16:3 (NIV).

Judea. Her character reappeared in her eldest son, Ahaziah, who, like his idolatrous mother, became a devout worshipper of Baal.

She became a treacherous schemer. The tragedy of Naboth and his vineyard revealed how despicable Jezebel became. Life seemed cheap to such a female who had murder in her veins. Her father, Ethbaal, murdered his predecessor.

Jezebel ordered by letter stamped with the royal seal a public feast. She also instituted an assembly of the people of Jezreel to try the pious Naboth for blasphemies against God and the king. Naboth was arrested, tried, and condemned on the false witnesses secured by Jezebel. She found these witnesses in order to appear within the bounds of the law. Found guilty, Naboth was stoned until his innocent life was beaten out of him. Then Ahab took possession of Naboth's vineyard.

Jezebel loved personal adornment. "The death of the one whom Jezebel had stirred up to work wickedness in the sight of the Lord" revealed her to be as incapable of remorse as of fear. There seemed no sign of repentance in her as she went out proudly to meet her prophesied doom. Jezebel's son and grandson met Jehu in the blood-stained vineyard Naboth had once possessed. Jehu slew Jezebel's son, the king of Israel. Her grandson was overtaken in flight and slain; the still proud, defiant queen-mother knew her last hour had come.

Jezebel died a horrible death. First, Jehu entered the city gate. Reaching the palace, he looked up to the window from which came the taunting voice of Jezebel: "Is it peace, thou Zimri, thou murderer of thy master?" Such a taunt maddened her victorious enemy, and seeing the two eunuchs standing at the window with the defiant queen, he shouted up to them, "Who is on my side? Who? Throw her down!"[124]

Second, they obeyed, and as she fell, the walls were sprinkled with her blood. Third, horses treaded her underfoot; and fourth, the hungry dogs wanted her flesh. Finally, the wicked Jezebel reaped what she sowed. Retribution had overtaken Jezebel when her body had been thrown out of the window to be torn and mangled, and then eaten by dogs. As a daughter of the devil, she suffered.

---

[124] 2 Kings 9:31–32 (NIV).

L. Deceitful Women of the Twenty-first Century

Mary Jo Eustace Case

I'm lying by the pool in Palm Springs, nursing my obligatory margarita, when I notice that my husband is nowhere in sight. In fact, I've been losing track of him all day. I do vaguely recall seeing him about an hour ago, but he was on his cell phone, earpiece planted firmly in place, pacing back and forth like a demented receptionist. I assumed he was talking to his agent, but I wasn't really sure. There had been a lot of phone calls since he joined us a few days ago on our little family vacation. Between the extended telephone time and the three-hour trips to the gym, I'd barely seen him at all. Now, usually I don't mind this sort of thing; most often, I welcome it. Being married as long as we have, alone time is actually a good thing. But this time, something seemed different.[125]

"Hey," I say.

"Hey," he answers in a numb tone.

I know instantly that something is wrong. He isn't looking me in the eye. In fact, he isn't looking at me at all. "What's the matter?"

"Nothing," he replies.

I decide to push. I can tell there is something wrong. "Just tell me." He turns to look at me and then decides to sleep on the floor instead. At that second, I knew. I knew it all. "Have you met someone?" He nods yes. I start to feel vaguely nauseous. I turn to the window, as if focusing on the horizon. "Is it Tori Spelling?" I turn around; he nods yes.

"Hey, what's up?" they ask. "Is everything okay?" I think of telling them, but realize if I do, it just might make it real. Instead, I nod and join my son a few steps away. I hug him and notice how golden he has become in the sun.

"Where's Daddy?" he asks.

I take a breath and tell him the first of many lies to come. I hate doing it. I hate Dean for making me do it. "Oh, he just left.

[125] Victoria Zackheim, *The Other Women* (New York: Warner Books, 2007), 15.

He had to go back and finish his movie." I look at him and search for a reaction. Could he tell I was lying? Did he hear a change in my voice and know that something earth-shattering had just happened? I heard that kids have a sixth sense about these things. I scan his face for cracks and secrets, but there are none. He smiles and gives me the biggest kiss ever and asks for a Shirley Temple. And for some reason, this is more than I can bear. It is such a normal request—something you ask for when your parents take you to a special place for dinner, or when you are on a family vacation. It was so innocent and so simple, and then it occurs to me that things would not be this innocent or simple for a very long time to come.

M. Diana Abu-Jaber Case

Notes began to appear under my office door with some regularity—about one or two a month—and occasionally they were folded and tucked in my department mailbox. Always just one line, often in question form: Why do you stay with him? Why don't you leave? Over time, they became more neutral, almost metaphysical. "Who are you?" asked one note. "Why are you even in my life?" asked another.[126]

After six months of watching this mystery girl misting past my office door, I had an idea of the caller's face. Her image came to me in pieces—eyes, hair, high heel—like a ransom note cut out of magazines. He ended up marrying a different woman, a nonstudent.

N. Susan Montez Case

"Let's go downstairs and talk, where we can take a walk." But Jewel was working up to hysteria. She had caught her husband with another woman, and she wanted to know what every woman always wanted to know: Who was she?

"It doesn't matter," Victor said. "It's not what you think."

[126] Zackheim, 246

She was crying and started yelling. "I'll go to the press. I'll wreck your career. I swear to God I will."

I sat in the dark bathroom musing that she might actually love him. I was even amazed that she was demonstrating signs of being genuinely hurt. On the other hand, I couldn't help thinking how funny it was that Jewel was causing such a scene because of me.

"Ha-ha," I thought to myself, "the older mistress triumphs over the young wife."

"I missed you," she yelled, "and I drove all the way up here in the rain to see you and you've got another woman locked in the bathroom. Who is it, Victor? Tell me who it is." Then there was a loud hang on the bathroom door. She alternately banged on the bathroom door and screamed at Victor.

He remained calm and kept asking her to go downstairs with him and let the bathroom occupant leave, but she wasn't having it. She wanted to know who her nemesis was. She wanted to know who was trying to steal her husband. "If I tell you who's here, will you let her leave and calm down?"

"Yes," she said.

O. Women's Movement

Christian views about women have varied for the last two thousand years.

Women were often excluded from leadership positions in the church. Midway through the twentieth century, and in some churches today, the church seemed unfavorable to woman pastoral positions. Women in some churches were overlooked and denied in many leadership roles. Women were also denied in government, society, and the family.

Throughout history, some Christians used the story of Adam and Eve to justify second-class status of women. Paul and early Christians looked to Adam and Eve's story to put the blame for the fall on Eve, concluding that women could not hold positions of authority or to teach.

At the turn of the twentieth century, women's social roles greatly expanded. Before then, most women's lives centered on their labor in the household taking care of the family, cooking, sewing, cleaning, and gardening.

Earlier, thousands of women felt trapped in bad marriages. Traditionalists were concerned that changes in sexual expectations may have led women to place their happiness above that of their husbands.[127] For better or worse, women decided what their limits were. Many unhappy couples gritted their teeth and tried to tough it out until the children left home. However, the stress of raising children placed a strain on even the happiest of marriages. Although Christianity seemed ambivalent about marriage, it also had a prohibition against divorce.

God's intention, Jesus said, was that a husband and wife became one flesh. "What therefore God hath joined together, let no man put asunder."[128]

P. Infidelity

When an affair exists, both partners feel as if their world had collapsed, wondering whether their marriage can survive. Few marital problems cause as much heartache and devastation as infidelity. Money worries, disagreement about children, or a serious illness placed a strain on the relationship. But because of the deep sense of betrayal, infidelity undermines the foundation of marriage itself is far more likely to lead to divorce than is any other issue. Nearly one in four married men and more than one in ten married women have had extramarital affairs—ranging from casual flings to long-term relationships with deep emotional attachments.

Ongoing emotional and physical relationships are hardest on a marriage. Despite these numbers, divorce doesn't have to be the inevitable resolution.

---

[127] Coonz, p. 204.

[128] The Holy Bible; NIV, Mk 10:19, Electronic.

Marriages can survive infidelity. With counseling, time, and a shared goal, some couples emerge from infidelity with a stronger and more honest relationship than before.[129]

Infidelity pointed to underlined problems in one's marriage. Not every marriage touched by infidelity should be saved. In some cases, too much damage may have occurred if both partners were not committed.[130]

Q. Divorce

Current divorce rates do not take into account conjugal dissolution rates occurring from cohabitations and the number of couples who separate but never divorce. The average duration of Canadian marriage ending in divorce in 2003 was 14.2 years, while in the United States it was 11 years for first marriages and 7.2 years for all marriages. The highest rate of divorce per 1,000 population occurs at the fourth anniversary when 26.2 of 1,000 marriages end in divorce (Ambert 2005). In 2002, the average age at divorce was 43 years for men and 40.5 years for women (Ambert 2005). It is a well-known fact that half of all divorces in the family life course occur in the first seven years of marriage (Cherlin 1981).[131]

It also appears that couples with highly educated parents run higher divorce risks, and they do so regardless of which spouse has parents with longer education (Lyngstad 2004). What are the consequences of divorce? The two most salient consequences are poverty and an increased risk for the development of problems among the children involved (Ambert 2005). For the first salient consequence, divorce is a dire cause of poverty for a large proportion of women and their children. Once separation takes place, the mother and child unit becomes even poorer. After divorce, women's household income decreases by about 20% to 40% while men's declines are less (Ambert 2005). Canada and the United States are the two western countries

[129] Mayo Clinic.com. (n.a., n.p.) updated 2006.

[130] Mayo Clinic.com. (n.a., n.p., n.d.).

[131] Document Page: "Marriage, Parenthood. Divorce Understanding the Past as We Move" (n.a., n.p., n.d.). http://elibrary.bigchalk.com

in which single-parent families experience extremely elevated poverty rates, and where there is a vast difference between the incomes of single- and two-parent families (Ambert 2005).[132]

While divorce appeared originally instituted to protect the sanctity of wedlock by outlawing the offender and his moral offense, and said granted only in case of adultery, it seemed most ludicrous to see how quickly people were divorced in recent years for trifling reasons.[133] Some marriages were being dissolved because the husband snored too much. The alarming increase in the divorce rate had disastrous effects upon the children of broken homes.

Jesus taught the indissolubility of thc marriagc union and affirmed that such was symbolic of the indissoluble union between himself and his church, just as the prophets spoke of monogamy, as symbolic of the union of God with Israel.[134] While Jesus recognized the Mosaic bill of divorcement, which declared adultery to be the sole reason of separation, he did not make divorce mandatory. Behind his teaching on this subject, it seemed to be the underlying principle that if a marriage became destroyed by unfaithfulness, it could not be further destroyed by divorce.[135]

R. The Damage of an Affair

The most damaged part of an affair seemed experienced by the victimized person. If a spouse or significant other were on the receiving end of infidelity, the most damaged part of this situation would be the lack of trust. Most persons would not come to grips with the infraction; however, resolving the potential of possible future infractions was where the people had the most damaged psychological effects.

[132] Ibid., 4.

[133] Matthew 5:32 (NIV).

[134] Isaiah 54:5; Jeremiah 3:14, 31:32; Hosea 2:19; Matthew 9:15 (NIV).

[135] Matthew 5:31 (NIV).

S. Conclusion

Looking at what biblical women did wrong helped women of the twenty-first century figure out how they should live right.[136] Women of the twenty-first century came to realize their differences from women of the Bible. Modern Christian women and biblical women shared many things, especially God.

On the other hand, women seemed active in the religious life of Israel throughout the Old Testament. In Jesus's treatment of women, women saw how God raised their position in life. He showed women compassion and respect in a way that woman had never known. Because of the Bible, women of modern times examined the Scripture as carefully as possible, in order to know God.

Biblical and women of the twenty-first century continued sharing some of the same experiences, although women of the twenty-first century have taken on more leadership roles. In many cases, destruction of the family continued because of disobedience, greed, lies, betrayal, murder, immoral sex, and deception. Eve's story proved women's inferior reasoning and deceit. Women used personal charm to lure men to destruction. When sin came into existence, divine retribution came into existence.

---

[136] Liz Curtis Higgs, *Bad Girls of The Bible and What We Can Learn from Them* (CO: WaterBrook Press, 1999), 174

WOMEN OF THE BIBLE VS. WOMEN OF THE TWENTY-FIRST CENTURY

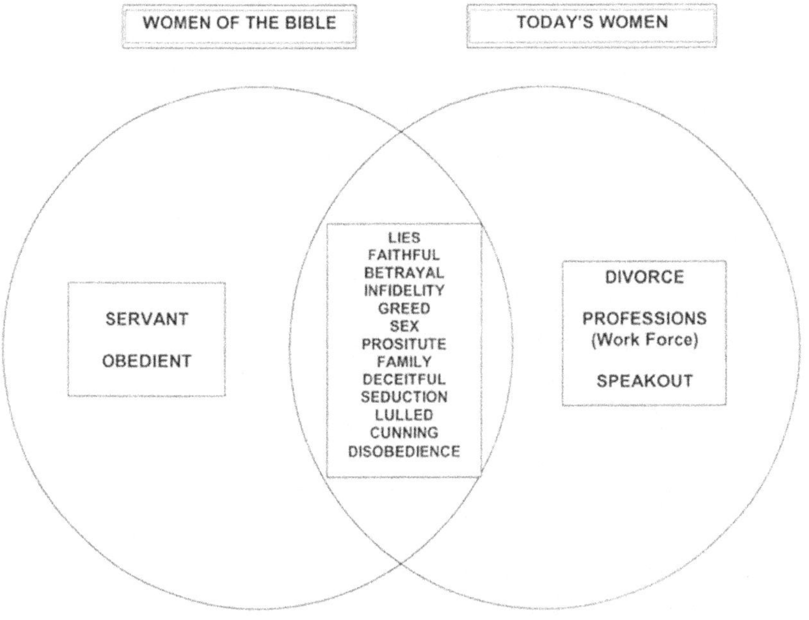

Chapter 6
Spiritual Women Explored Appropriate Strategies that Work in World Missions

A. Introduction

Approximately 27 percent of the world's population remained unevangelized and without a local body of believers to share the good news of the Gospel. For people living in those cultures, even if the unsaved wanted to know more about a god who loved them, there was no one in their culture pointing them to God. The unsaved need someone from outside to come in as an evangelist. Yet, there was a great imbalance in current missionary efforts. Three percent of the missionary workforce was unreached. In 2000, Christian organizations in the United States spent $269 billion ministering to Christians and evangelizing non-Christians.

In the same year, Christian organizations spent $810 million for ministry to unevangelized non-Christians, a mere 0.3% of the total.[137] Today spiritual women explored different strategies that could work in world missions.

[137] Document Perspective on World Christian Movement, http://find galegroup.com (n.a., p. 1, 2007).

B. The Greatest Need

In recognition of the changes of challenges of world missions, many women leaders have moved from a missionary-oriented approach to a missionsoriented approach. Working with US agencies and national partners in the international church, churches should provide resources, human and financial support of global evangelism, and church planting effort in strategic areas of the world. Spiritual leaders had strategically invested their people and their resources in key areas of the world to introduce lost people to Jesus Christ. This enabled them to become fully devoted followers of Christ.

"Therefore go and make disciples of all nations, baptizing them in the name of the Father and of the Son and of the Holy Spirit, and teaching them to obey everything I have commanded you."[138]

C. New Opportunities and Strategies in World Missions

The era of the western church being the leader in world missions is ending as the international church is actively increasing its role in global evangelism and church planting. Already there are more people joining the missionary force from newer sending countries like Brazil, Nigeria, Singapore, and Korea than from longtime leaders Canada and the United States. The international church movement primarily needs resources: human and financial. Human resources are needed to assist with evangelism, biblical education, leadership, and special skills training so that individual churches, church movements, and ministries can become indigenously led and reproducing. Financial resources are needed to help these churches, church movements, and ministries become self-sustaining. The church in America, rich in these resources, is being called to new strategies of partnership with the international churches.[139]

---

138 Matthew 28:19–20 (NIV).

139 *New Opportunities and Strategies*, http://find.galegroup.com (n.a., p. 3, 2009).

D. Mobilization of Missionaries

Education and exposure to and participation in cross-cultural ministry opportunities would encourage each missionary to explore his or her role in expanding God's kingdom. Examples should include projects in international communities in the local areas and short-term trips to culturally different locations.

E. Geographic Strategy

Spiritual women should target a specific geographic region in the world where they could make a significant impact. This region should become characterized by strategic needs in the areas of evangelism, national church assistance, socioeconomic problems, and by a positive response to the Gospel.

Priorities

Priorities would guide the unsaved in decision-making and in the investment of their people and their financial resources.

1. Overseas evangelism and church planting among least-reached peoples provided support for existing missionaries, national workers and churches, new missionaries, and organizations.
2. Overseas training—support for personnel, organizations, and projects should be offered for national church leaders.
3. Support for personnel, organizations, and projects would assist evangelism, church planting, discipleship, and caring for the people as a whole. Healthcare specialists, teachers, pilots, technicians, agriculturists, administrators, Bible translators, and missionary care personnel should all be included in evangelism.
4. Consideration should be given to global ministry opportunities arising from political, social, or economic changes that would provide special occasions for the spread of the Gospel.

F. Defining People Groups

For evangelization purposes, a people group is the largest group within which the Gospel can spread as a church planting movement without encountering barriers of understanding or acceptance.[140]

In most parts of the world, lack of understandability acted as the main barrier, and it became appropriate to define people group primarily by language, with the possibility of subdivisions based on dialect or cultural variations. Such a list would be referred to as an ethno-linguistic list of peoples.[141]

In other parts of the world, it had been noted that acceptance was a greater barrier than understandability.

Ideally, people group would always be defined to mean (a) all individuals in the group understand each other reasonably well and (b) cultural relationship barriers aren't so high that the transmission of the Gospel is seriously impeded.[142]

G. Defining People Groups by the Highest Barrier

An argument can be made for defining "people group" according to the highest of the two barriers (understandability and acceptance), in some circumstances. If understandability is the most important barrier, then a linguistic, or an ethno-linguistic, approach is used. With this approach, one people group doesn't speak more than one language (apart from occasional bilingual individuals), although more than one people group may speak a given language if cultural or dialect differences warrant. In most of the world, this is the approach we use.[143]

---

[140] What is a People Group? http://www.joshuaproject.net (n.a., n.p., 2009).

[141] What is a People Group? (n.a., n.p., 2009).

[142] What is a People Group? (n.a., n.p., 2009).

[143] What is a People Group? (n.a., n.p., n.d.).

H. Be Innovative and Flexible

There were many different models or forms a successful cross-cultural women's ministry could take. There was no right structure. Some groups had moved toward Anglo-American forms, but none would go all the way. This bothered some churches. But it should not. Christians believed that God created diversity. Some said, if they're going to live here, why don't they learn English, but this question revealed a prideful heart. They were really asking, when were they going to become like them? Two congregations could meet in the same building, worship in different languages and cultural adaptations, and still be united in Jesus Christ (Eph. 4:3–6). Christians should be willing to go everywhere, and anywhere, to proclaim the true gospel of Christ.[144]

Organizational unity was not the same as spiritual unity. It seemed to be a common human trait to expect everyone to be exactly as they were. Yet, the goal was seeking and saving that which was lost. Organization was a means, not a goal.

Sometimes complete integration of distinct ethnic groups happens in time. But it cannot be programmed. The molding of church worship forms, schedule, and style will be a product of felt needs under the guidance of the Bible and the Holy Spirit. One's goal must be to provide an atmosphere that will allow local people to accept Christ and live out their Christian lives in the patterns of the local society, in the style most natural to them. Sunday school classes and sermons can nurture attitudes of tolerance and openness. Explore the strong biblical themes that the Church is responsible to reach all nations for Christ, and that all nations will be represented around the throne.

Explore Jesus's question, "Who is my neighbor?"[145]

Congregational involvement. Missions-mobilizing churches in this international age are actively involved in their missions' works.

---

[144] Mark Mittelberg, 59.

[145] How to Start a Cross-Cultural Ministry at Your Church. http://find.galegroup.com (o.a., p. I, 2009).

Not only do they support long-term missionaries who know the languages and cultures of the people among whom they minister, they also coordinate short-term campaigns to their mission points that develop horizons for missions and evangelism within the local church.

Congregational involvement, however, should vary depending on the maturity of developing movements. In young movements the local church should *serve* as *senders.* In *Serving* as *Senders*, Neal Pirolo says that for every soldier on the frontline of battle, nine provide support for him.

Churches stand behind their missionaries by providing (1) moral, (2) logistic, (3) financial, (4) prayer, (5) communication, and (6) reentry support (Pirolo 1991). After the first churches are established, the sending church begins to *serve as encouragers* of a young movement. They encourage missionaries and new Christians by email, letters, and telephone calls. They also encourage by field visits that provide hands-on expressions of compassion and solidarity. For example, members of the sending church might help construct a church building or provide health and medical needs to those living in poverty. As missions churches grow to maturity, the sending church should *serve* as *resources* for the developing movement. Elders interact with elders about the nature of shepherding; evangelists reflect with evangelists about becoming a missions-mobilizing movement; youth from both cultures encourage one another in the Lord. Active involvement by the missions-mobilizing church includes short-term workers laboring beside tong-term workers, according to the gifts given to the body.[146]

Although women played a significant role in world missions, few studies have been done to ascertain what factors enhanced their effectiveness and sense of well-being.

Female missionaries have been a neglected population both in the writing of mission history and in empirical studies in the field of mental health. Some mission organizations, however, are beginning

[146] Nancy Crawford and Helen M. Devries, "Relationship Between Role Perception and Well-Being in Married Female," http://find.gale group.com (2005), 188.

to recognize the unique challenges facing female missionaries and are seeking to better enable and care for them. Concurrently, several studies have empirically confirmed the existence of significant distinctive experiences of female and male missionaries (Adams & Clopton 1990; Carter 1999; Chester 1983; Gish 1983; Strickland 1990; Wilcox 1995). These studies have underscored the importance of understanding the experiences of female missionaries so as to better support them in their work and to enhance their well-being.[147]

A recent study by Hall and Duvall (2003), examined a range of markers for well-being (e.g., energy level, satisfaction with life, mood, etc.) and compared the scores of female missionaries who had a direct or support ministry role with ones who were homemakers. They found that the homemakers reported being more relaxed and less anxious and tense than the other groups and reported higher levels of wellbeing than did the others. Additionally, they found a correlation between wives' actual ministry roles and self-expectations of their ministry roles with their self-assessment of well-being. In other words, those wives who had no discrepancy between the actual role and the desired role had more positive well-being. These findings suggest that the freedom to choose the role one has (whether direct ministry, support ministry, or homemaker) is a key factor in the well-being of married female missionaries.[148]

One striking theme of these and other studies focusing on missionary wives and mothers is a suggested relationship between the woman's ministry role and well-being. Specifically, the following themes have been suggested from this review of the literatures: (a) Married female missionaries without adequate education may experience loss of a meaningful role after their children are out of the home (Beck 1986); (b) married female missionaries may express satisfaction with their ministry role, but may have low levels of wellbeing (Adams & Clopton 1990; English 1995); (c) the married female missionary's work/role satisfaction is a primary reason MK educators remain (Wilcox 1995); (d) one of the restraints to ministry activity

---

[147] Ibid., 188.
[148] Ibid., 189.

for a married female missionary is her need to develop a role within the setting of her husband's work (Cocks 1997); and (e) congruence between the role one has and one's desired role is key to well-being (Hall & Duvall 2003).[149]

The above literature provided evidence for the importance of a woman's perceived ministry role and her own well-being, as well as her willingness to extend her service. This became necessary in order to assess the well-being of married female missionaries.

Through sermons, prayer meetings, weekly and monthly periodicals devoted to missionary progress, memoirs, and biographies of returned missionaries, and anniversary meetings at which the unsaved and native converts would speak, the missionary spirit extended beyond the church to infuse urban culture more generally.

Congregational missions and the making of an imperial culture should have drawn upon the rich documentation of them missionary society. There should have been discussions about the relationships between home and between ideas of race and class. The poor at home and the heathen should have seen the significance of missions in enabling the extension of the women of the twenty-first century's role. However, the mission's landscape shifted.

South Korea sent 34 percent of its missionaries to unreached people groups, and many of the missionaries went directly from churches and received no support from denominational agencies. One pastor, Samuel Kang, led an ambitious twenty-five-year plan to help South Korea send out more missionaries than any other country. South Korean Christians were ambitious, and they were determined to share the gospel throughout the world.[150]

Other non-Western countries stepped up their missions efforts. In 1973, just over 3,400 non-Western, cross-cultural missionaries served on mission fields.

In 2006, that number had grown to 103,000. The day of western missionary dominance came to an end.

---

[149] Allison Twells, *Congressional Missions and the Making of an Imperial Culture in Nineteenth-century England*, http://find.galegroup.com (2002) 1.

[150] Nancy Crawford and Helen M. Devries, 187.

While Baptists should have celebrated the work of South Korean and other non-Western Christians, they recommitted themselves to the work of missions.

It was difficult to imagine the pain, mistrust, and alienation those women must have continued to feel. Women of the twenty-first century should create an out pouring of loving support to assist in the healing process for each individual.

Female missionaries (women of the twenty-first century) had been a neglected population both in writing of mission history and in studies in the field of mental health. Some mission organizations, however, recognized the unique challenges facing women of the twenty-first century missionaries and were determined to seek better care for them. Concurrently, several studies have empirically confirmed the existence of significant distinctive experiences of female and male missionaries (Adams & Clopton 1990; Carter 1999; Chester 1983; Gish 1983; Strickland 1990; Wilcox 1995). These studies have underscored the importance of understanding the experiences of female missionaries in order to support them better in their work and to enhance their *well-being*. The sending of women of the twenty-first century missionaries proved not a single process; it involved a lot of hard work, dedication, and determination.

I. Recruiting

Perhaps the most important part of the recruitment task of women of the twenty-first century was determining what sources would be emphasized. At first, local churches and denominational councils were the primary arena for the recruitment of missionary candidates. Having moved away during twenty-first century from the local approach because of the need for large-scale coordination, the pendulum was swinging back to local churches, especially larger ones. Every church was driven by something.

J. Selecting

The steadily more assertive posture of women of the twenty-first century mission had centered on the issue of appropriateness for given sorts of missionary service. Across the past two hundred years, and especially as mission agencies became more noticeable in their managerial and technological functions, screening of potential personnel became much more pervasive. The difficulty of assessing spiritual gifts and the pressure to deploy younger missionaries caused a shift from literal biblical criteria in favor of measurable competencies and traits.

K. Deploying

Formal corporate decision-making about locations and situations wherein missionaries may have been productive, over against the more opened approach (wherever God calls), had longed been a tension in mission management. To a greater extent than many missionaries were prepared to accept, the mission agency usually had a determinative role in the decisions about where to station missionaries, what work to do, and how to allocate project funds and technical support. As the role of the mission agency became steadily more proactive and determinative, this source of conflict created a sharp division between those who made choices and those who relied on intuitive and inspirational feelings about the leading of God. The global goal should have been its international partnerships in missions. Organizations should have taken adequate account of the upsurge of local-church participation and missionary initiatives. Evangelism brought new converts to spiritual maturity as they continued to grow.

L. Accountability

Women of the twenty-first century should affix accountability of the missionaries by urging or requiring some sort of periodic review of financial and job-related performances. While some women missionaries resented any accountability other than directly to God, the experiences of totally independent women missionaries demonstrated the need for accountability. Tensions today increased the technological and nature of managerial oversight, represented by standardized report forms, formal travel reports (rarely used by leaders as a basis of informed interaction with the missionary), and busywork procedures, such as required preapproval of events and expenditures.

M. Management

Managing missionaries of the twenty-first century and their mission projects became a prerogative usually assumed by the mission agency and often delegated to selected missionary councils or leadership groups on the field. The larger the financial exposure or risk, the more likely the missionaries were to take dominant responsibility.

N. Reporting

Women of the twenty-first century communications fell into two categories: from the missionary to his or her own immediate supporters, and from the agency to those same supporters plus the agency's own list of contributors and churches, corporate sponsors, and large-scale donors. Many agencies for missionaries have moved more directly into campaigning for funds through various sorts of centrally distributed devices banks, pledges, and book sales.

O. Intermediacy

Limited communications and the time it had taken to travel great distances could have left a great load on missionaries and the mission agency.

Missionaries became the carrier of this burden. One aspect was the need to represent the mission and its missionaries to governments and regulatory agencies. Everything from immigration and naturalization regulations, to passports, visas, residency permits, taxes, school loans, and the many dozens of other hidden tasks required time and skills, which, realistically, were best provided by the agency, in hope to improve the women of the twenty-first century missions.

P. Support

Mission boards and executive officers should have taken the responsibility in assisting the unsaved by encouraging prayer, support, and exhorting the immediate constituencies in maintaining and expanding the missions' financial support. Many women of the twenty-first century missionaries participated in this process with more or less help from their mission agencies. The entire responsibility was sometimes carried by the agency, especially within the larger denominations.

Q. African American Baptist Women Missionaries of the Twenty-first Century

African American Baptist women of the twenty-first century pioneered in the great work in Christian missions. These women established a record of leadership in the National Baptist Convention, USA, Inc. (NBC-USA), and the Lott Carey Baptist Foreign Mission Convention. The African American missionary tradition derived from the eighteenth-century evangelism that stressed that God dealt directly with the individual and that all faithful Christians had a sacred duty to share their faith with others. Missionary work was be characterized by two dimensions: (1) the spiritual dimension, which described those Christians who attempted to convert other people through religious instruction and preaching, and (2) the temporal dimension, which identified the work of those Christians performing tasks of a humanitarian nature such as providing their charges with an education or medical care. In the nineteenth century, African American Baptist women who served on foreign mission fields worked as nurses, teachers, and preachers. Others performed even greater tasks.[151]

---

[151] Beverly Guy-Sheftall, *Daughters of Sorrow: Attitudes Toward Black Women* (New York: Carlson Publishing Co., 1990), 155.

Louise "Lulu" Fleming was born a slave in Hibernia Clay County, Florida, on January 28, 1862. She graduated from Shaw University in 1885 and left the United States two years later for the mission field. Assigned to Palabala, Congo, by the Woman's Baptist Foreign Missionary Society of the West, her initial charge was to teach primary classes in English. Returning to the United States in 1892, because of declining health, she realized that she needed to make a way out of no way, and thus, Fleming enrolled in the Leonard Medical School and subsequently completed the medical course at Philadelphia's Woman's Medical College. In addition to teaching, Fleming could then provide much needed medical care to the people she was to serve in the mission field.[152]

Nora Antonio Gordon, the daughter of two former slaves, also dedicated her life to foreign missions. She entered Spelman Seminary in 1882 and graduated in 1888, and under the auspices of the Woman's Baptist Missionary Society. She too was assigned to the Congo after additional training as a missionary. Although Gordon taught Sunday school and day classes, her ideas were similar to those held by members of early black women's clubs. These women of the twenty-first century emphasized the teaching of good morals to black women and girls. Gordon wrote, "If we can save women, girls and have intelligent Christian wives and mothers, it would change the entire atmosphere of the community."[153]

National Baptist Women Missionaries in Liberia in the 1920s, Jeannine DeLombard presented the story of three early twentieth century women: Emma Bertha Delaney, Susie Taylor, and Eliza Davis. These women established missions and schools in Liberia, which grew into flourishing institutions within ten years. Delaney founded Suehn Industrial Mission in Montserrado County, Liberia, in 1912, using land donated by the Liberian government. Because of limited resources, she was compelled to make a way out of no way. She raised a substantial amount of money to support the school while she was on furlough in the United States. Delaney also established sewing

[152] Ibid., 155.

[153] Guy-Sheftall, 20.

classes and a women's society in Malawi. In establishing their school, Susie Taylor and Eliza Davis performed intense physical labor. They cleared the land of trees and other vegetation themselves so that the Baptist Industrial Academy in Liberia could be constructed. With few resources or no resources, these women made a way out of no way.[154]

Being a missionary woman in the foreign field would have been no easy task during the nineteenth century, but by the end of the twentieth century, missionaries had access to new technology, more advanced medical care, and thus, their work was perhaps not as difficult. A twentieth-century female missionary, Shirley Russell, who later became an ordained minister of Pittsburgh's Ebenezer Baptist Church, spent twelve years serving in Haiti during the tumultuous Baby Doc Duvalier dictatorship. While there, Russell observed the mistreatment of many people. The political circumstances of women heading leadership roles back then did not allow her to say or preach anything except Jesus Christ. Nor could she verbalize any negative criticism of the Haitian government without incurring possible retaliation. Clearly understanding the political climate and the restrictions, Russell assumed her charge as a missionary.

Many African American Baptist women of the twenty-first century in foreign missions focused their work on education and medical care. They paid close attention to the needs of women. Russell's emphasis, however, was on children. She founded an orphanage in Port-au-Prince, Haiti, called it the Love Center Mission. The mission provided children with a safe place to sleep and it fed and clothed the orphans. The mission's goal was to take the children out of darkness [and] into the marvelous light. An already existing, two-story structure was purchased, and the new orphanage was equipped with a pharmacy and a huge kitchen. Russell recalled that she had forty-three children in the orphanage and eventually almost two hundred. "Sometimes, I would wake up in the mornings to find children on the doorstep with a note attached to them."[155]

---

[154] Ibid., 21.

[155] Ibid., 155.

Russell realized that as a twenty-first century American she had everything compared to many people in Haiti, but as a missionary, she felt compelled to adapt to her environment. Russell ate the same food she served the orphans, but when she drank the same water, she became quite ill. This setback was only a minor one for Russell because Ebenezer Baptist Church in Pittsburgh, Pennsylvania, soon began providing additional support for the Haiti mission stat on by ensuring a weekly delivery of water by truck.

While in Haiti, Russell realized that there were significant religious differences between the twenty-first century Christianity she proclaimed and the faith of the Haitian people, but she refused to make any adjustments on her part. God sent her there to introduce those bound in voodoo to Jesus Christ, and many of the Haitians believe in voodoo like women of the twenty-first century we believe in Jesus Christ. Preaching the Gospel among Haitians once resulted in her being kidnapped, and her life was threatened.

The Haitian women whom she tried to help conspired against her, and she was physically snatched, placed into a car, and forced to sit at a table all night.

During that night, she focused on prayer, and the next day, she was released. Her life was spared. Russell was driven to a location where she could find her way back to Port-au-Prince, where she later attributed her safe arrival back at the orphanage to Jesus, the way maker.

R. No Greater Mission

Women of the twenty-first century who were followers of Christ had a mission. These women had a life-transformed message to proclaim to those who needed to hear it. Every day, people all over the world were being saved from sin and its consequences through faith in the Lord Jesus. Women of the twentyfirst century's mission as his followers were to be messengers who preached the Gospel of peace, telling others about the Savior, Jesus Christ.

S. What Was a Missionary?

Jesus said to them again, "As the Father has sent Me, I also send you."[156]

A missionary was someone sent by Jesus Christ just as he was sent by God. The great controlling factor should not be the needs of people but the command of Jesus. The source of Jesus inspiration in missionary service for God would have been behind, not ahead of the missionaries. The tendency today was to sweep everything together in front of peoples' lives and make it conformed to their definition of success. But in the New Testament, the inspiration had been put behind himself. The goal was to be true to Jesus—to carry out his plans.

Personal attachment to the Lord Jesus and to his perspective should have never been overlooked. In missionary work, the great danger was that God's call could be replaced by the needs of the people, to the point that human sympathy for those needs would absolutely overwhelm the meaning of being sent by Jesus. The needs appeared so enormous, and the conditions so difficult, that every power of the mind faltered and failed. Women tended to forget that the reason underneath all missionary work was not primarily the elevation of the people, their education, nor their needs, but first and foremost the command of Jesus Christ—"Go therefore and make disciples of all the nations…" (Matt. 28:19).[157]

According to many women, there were several mission agencies, and no two were alike. Mission agencies differed in terms of what their primary vision was, where they focused their missionary efforts, whether they served the whole body of Christ in general or a single denomination, and what kind of organizational structure existed.

Some agencies focused on only one kind of ministry. For example, some focused only on literature production and distribution, whereas others focused on Bible translation, radio outreach, or ministry to youth, etc. Some agencies *concentrated on one geographical*

[156] John 20:21 (NIV).

[157] Matthew 28:19 (NIV).

region or people group. Other agencies served only one denomination. To have been the agency deployed with them, they would belong to that denomination. Where some agencies were highly structured, with high standards to join, others were informal in their design.

Missions of the women of the twenty-first century should exist to serve the entire body of Christ, regardless of denominational affiliation.

Organizationally, these missions were operated with as little structure as possible, trying to balance the need for support and accountability of women missionaries with the purpose to release Christians to do God's work. Some missionaries worked independently, where others worked pointer-in-pointer with US-based churches and other mission agencies.

T. Why Were Mission Agencies Needed?

From New Testament times when Paul's apostolic band left on its first missionary journey, the church had created structures to serve the needs of people who were called by God into the ministry. These organizations—whose members were not only committed Christians but were also involved in full-time service—existed solely to serve ministers and missionaries. Just as a local church served the needs of its members, those organizations served missionaries and ministers.

Women of the twenty-first-century mission should provide services that would be difficult for an individual local church to provide consistently. The missions provides standardized candidate approval process, financial legal and tax consultant services, promotion of missionary projects to an international audience, informational resources to missionaries about new trends, and other things related to missions. They also provided assistance in printing and mailing monthly newsletters, maintenance of mailing lists, travel scheduling, communication with supporters, and of course, the monthly receiving and distribution of financial support from thousands of individuals, churches, businesses, and other organizations nationwide, etc.

Without the involvement of local churches, missions would not exist. Local churches should provide the support base for global missions.

Relationally, churches had been encouraged to maintain strong ties with the missionaries they supported. Through letters, phone calls, and email messages, relationships should be nurtured across the miles. Pastoral counsel, ministry to the family, support for special events, assistance with furloughs, visits to the field, involvement with projects on the field, and dialogue with church leaders about special needs should have been encouraged.

George Miley wrote in his book (*Loving the Church*) that he strongly believed that a Christian community enabled a powerful worship. He felt that worship was the intricate part of the mission, and he strongly believed that this Christian community created a reason to utilize each other's gift. He referred to the church as an earthly body. He also reiterated that rediscovering God's plan became a critical issue that the mission's movements had faced throughout the world.[158]

On the other hand, John Piper stated in his book (*Let the Nations Be Glad*) missions were not God's only goal, worship became the ultimate goal. He insisted that the only reason that missions existed were because worship had not.[159] He stated that worship was the fuel for the missions. This simply implied that missions or worship could be effective without the other.

Howard Foltz stated in his book (*Healthy Churches in a Sick World*) Christians should develop an active consistent systematic ministry in order to nourish the needs of the world. He stated that one sure way to have an impact on the world was to silence Satan with God's word and continue to follow God in his glory while Christians used his/her gifts and talents.[160]

---

[158] George Miley, *Loving the Church in a Sick World, Blessing the Nations: Pursuing the Role of Local Churches in Global Missions* (OR: Gabriel Publishing Co., 2003), 59.

[159] John Piper, *Let the Nations Be Glad* (MI: Baker Books, 2003), 20.

[160] Howard Foltz, *Healthy Churches in a Sick World* (CA: Xulon Press, 2002), 167.

In Global News Howard Snyder believed that all of God's people were shaped in part by Christians' world views. They touched every dimension of life socially, educationally, economically, politically, and religiously. Snyder went on to say people's different views accounted for many of the Christians living styles, thinking, speaking, and images that existed among cultures and communities.[161]

U. Conclusion

Recent research on women in the twenty-first century in missions has enabled people and deepened people's understanding of the overall impact of Christians. At this same time, research had drawn attention to the contributions of thousands of women. Although women at first played a relatively minor role in the leadership and decision-making processes of most mission societies, their presence had been nonetheless vital to the work of missions and even today was recognized as such.

Despite the recognition of the research about women of the twenty-first century missions, there was still relatively few studies of women who were influential or prominent in mission service in comparison with the number of studies chronicling the lives of their male counterparts. The work of women missionaries helped researchers examine important processes such as conversion, the impact of the social gospel, and historical changes in gender relations, particularly as Christians related to the place of women in the Christian church today.

As missionaries, women purposes should have been to preach the Christian Gospel. Women of the twenty-first century not only had strong beliefs in God, but they also had strong opinions on the issues of their day. Their beliefs occasionally placed them at odds with their male colleagues and their mission society.

Despite the women of the twenty-first century missionaries' enthusiasm for the work that lay ahead, they received sharp criticism.

---

[161] Howard Snyder, *Global Good News: Mission in a New Context* (TN: Abingdon Press, 2001), 191.

These women had decided to act on their convictions that they were equal to men both in mission service and in Christian religious practice. Women volunteered for work few men were willing to undertake. They placed themselves in a region where they were beyond the protection of their government's consular services.

In fact, not even the possibility of assistance from the government existed where local warlords had absolute power. Their safety in what became an increasingly unsettled region ultimately depended on the goodwill of the local population. Without it, these women would never travel as many miles and for such a long period as they did.

The travels of these women provided a strong argument for sending women, as well as men, to work in the northwest of China. As they would make clear in their books and articles, no male missionary, however sincere or well regarded by the local people, could interact with Muslim women as they did. Invitations to women's quarters allowed the three British women to meet local women in their homes and to visit the same women regularly throughout their time in the northwest. In short, women were vital to the success of any Christian effort in the Muslim regions.[162]

The travels of women in Muslim regions brought women missionaries another form of fame, which most missionaries neither aspired to nor had the energy or ability to pursue.

Energetic twentieth-century North American women missionaries helped build a global church with majority female membership, despite widespread social and theological misgivings about women serving as evangelists. In this strong and inclusive collection, based partly on a Boston University seminar series, Dana Robert draws together research taking up where her own pioneering overview of the period in American Women in Mission (1997) left off.[163]

---

[162] Ted Ward, *Recent Trends and Baptist Missions*, http://find.galegroup.com (1999) 6.

[163] Deborah Gaitskell, *Gospel Bearers. Gender Barriers*, http://find.galegroup.com (2004) 43.

Chapter 7
The Sovereignty of God

A. Introduction

The reason this topic had been selected was because women of the Bible felt it was pertinent for women of the twenty-first century to understand salvation. Women of the twenty-first century (God's children) welcomed that glorious invitation to the Lord's Supper, from the Holy One, something, that biblical women and women of the twenty-first century had honored.

Women of the twenty-first century faced probably the most important questions of all: Just exactly, what did Jesus's death accomplish? How did it solve the problems of sin? Salvation! Salvation was when God rescued women from themselves as well as others, then he delivered them from that deadly thing known as sin, and finally, Jesus restored these women in complete spiritual health.[164]

Women of the Bible would remind women of the twenty-first century about how God overcame that alienation, which sin caused and restored them to a condition of peace. Sin was a willful reflection of God's reign and therefore it lead to some serious consequences. It was crucial that Christian women knew about God's plan. Could God's plan be the reason so many women of the twenty-first century became better spiritual leaders today?

[164] Psalm 23:3 (NIV).

B. Predestination

Some women of the twenty-first century believed that a person who accepted salvation or made a commitment to Christ would ultimately *be* saved, no matter how that person lived or what that people decided on later in life. This decision guaranteed it. *Wrong!* According to the author Pink (*The Sovereignty of God*), God gave people the freedom to come with respect to him. God did not force salvation on anyone who decided he did not want it. The Bible warned Christians about the danger of falling away from salvation.[165] Peter insisted that those who returned to their sinful ways after knowing Christ were worse off than before.[166] Those facts confirmed that women of the twenty-first century should not play with God. Women of the Bible would warn women of today that their salvation lay totally in the character of God and in what women had accomplished through Jesus Christ. God was eager and excited with a desire to save fallen human beings.[167]

Women of the Bible would tell women of the twenty-first century that God's predestination was part of his plan. When Peter wrote that Christians are chosen according to the foreknowledge of God the Father,[168] he was aware that this was all part of God's will. Whatever God did, he did it for a reason. He made it known that he would accomplish his work with or without man.

Everything that existed was because of God. He allowed it and called it into existence.

Biblical women would tell women of today that God knew the future, the past, and the present. God decided the destination of each of them. His predetermining decision was based on his will. Pink spoke about the human's heart and how grace acted first on it to awaken a person's desire to do God's will. God had blessed women of today with every spiritual blessing in Christ, just as he had chosen women of the Bible in him before the foundations of the world.

---

[165] Hebrews 6:4–6 (NIV).

[166] 2 Peter 2:20 (NIV).

[167] 1 Timothy 2:4 (NIV).

[168] 1 Peter 1:1–2 (NIV).

God being an all-loving God knew that women were dead in their transgressions and made women alive together with Christ, and raised them up with him.[169] Yet, there were those women that questioned God's absolute sovereignty.

Many women of the twenty-first century have had a hard time comprehending that God was not the author of sin. However, he did allow sin! God did not force women to do anything. If this was the case, many women would not be here today. There was none like him! Sometimes it had taken evil things to happen in peoples' lives to remind them that it was God that should be glorified, not man.

Women of the twenty-first century should be held accountable for their relationship with God and the decisions that they made in regards to the Gospel. Women of the Bible would point out to women of today that rejecting God was rejecting wisdom, hope, peace, love, and life itself. Jesus knew of the people that would reject him. He reminded people that it was the will of God who sent him, that everyone who believed in him would have life forever.

Women of the Bible would ask the women of today, how could they reject God's invitation to eternal life? Women of the Bible would say women of the twenty-first century owe God the highest praise. This was a way of acknowledging that God was God, and through him all things were possible. At the same time women of the Bible had affirmed that it was all the work of the Master.

What really stood out in women of today's mind was that they were abundantly blessed because the Father of their Lord had blessed all with such blessings in him even before the foundations of the world. Paul cried out with an overwhelming joy for people possessions in Christ. The fact that God had chosen women after all the sin they committed was miraculous! He chose them! There were so many women of today that did not want to be around their children and yet, Jesus adopted women of the Bible and women of the twenty-first century out of a love that no person could ever imagine. What a mighty God Christians serve.

---

[169] Romans 8:28–30 (NIV).

C. Holy Communion

Biblical women would say that God sought personal obedience and lifelong relationships with women of the twenty-first century. The teacher along with MacArthur knew that they were blessed in the fellowship of with Christians sharing that precious faith! Pink had spoken of the joy that filled his body when he was about to celebrate Communion with his congregation. Biblical women would insist that Communion represented a special meal that recalled the fellowship Jesus shared with his twelve disciples, in particular the Last Supper on the night before his death. This was a very special time because of the joyous act of Thanksgiving for all that the Father had done for everyone. It was an honor to participate in this blessed occasion.

Biblical women would inform the women of today that according to scripture this was instituted by Jesus. It was an honor to partake in this ritual every month, knowing that people were doing it in remembrance and in respect for Jesus, for giving his life for a sinner like them.[170] Women of the Bible would warn women of the twenty-first century that this was essential out of respect for Jesus.

Although many women of the twenty-first century interpreted the Last Supper in many different ways, it continued to represent the body and the blood of Jesus Christ. The most obvious reason of the Lord's Supper was memory. According to Apostle Paul, Jesus said, "Do this in remembrance of me," once as he broke the bread and second as he passed the wine.[171] This immediately placed Jesus's death in a sacrificial perspective, focusing Christian's attention on his death in honor of his memory.

Biblical women warned women of the twenty-first century that the Lord's Supper promoted a sense of fellowship among the members of a church family. What was so amazing about it was that people should have made things right with God before participating in it, although there were some people that did not honor this.

---

[170] Matthew 26:29 (NIV).

[171] Matthew 26:29 (NIV).

What a way to demonstrate God's love for everyone when Jesus held up the cup and stated that the cup was a symbol of his blood for the forgiveness of their sins and that the bread represented his broken body for the remission of peoples' sins. Jesus did all of this through his grace. What a price to pay for someone so undeserving, sinners. Biblical women would say to women of the twenty-first century that women owed God, the one that emancipated his children, forgave them, and then adopted them as his very own. What an unpayable debt!

Many women of the twenty-first century had asked, why did Jesus do all of this? Well, Pink and MacArthur made the answers to this question very short, sweet, simple, and straight to the point with triple C's. They were probably calm, cool, and *collective* as they replied, because "He wanted to!"

D. The Holy Spirit

Women of twenty-first century realized that because of Jesus's shed blood, they were bought with a price. This conveyed God's purpose for a person's life (his will). If this was not enough, he elected women, embraced women, protected women, loved women, and then he turned right around and forgave women. He offered Christians an inheritance from him if they remained in him.[172] A question women of the Bible would have for women of the twenty-first century would be, what was their reaction when Jesus implied that he had to leave? This was when God reminded women of the twenty-first century of the Comforter (Holy Spirit) that Jesus left behind to dwell within them for guidance and direction. Think of the passion and the zeal Paul felt knowing that he was being led by the Holy Spirit. Paul probably was impressed. He urged people to be guided by the Spirit of God who saved them. Thank you, Jesus!

Blessed was the God and Father of our Lord Jesus Christ, who had blessed people with every spiritual blessing in the heavenly places in Christ.[173] God gave women of the Bible and women of the twen-

[172] Ephesians 1:14 (NIV).
[173] Ephesians 1:3 (NIV).

ty-first century insight to hear his message of truth, to hear the gospel of salvation, and to believe. Biblical women knew that there was absolutely no way of gaining access to that hope Jesus spoke about without the Holy Spirit. This was probably why the Lord's Table was not for everyone. If people were not a Christian, celebration was not for them! The fact of the matter was that if women of the twenty-first century did not know Christ, they could not appreciate the redemptive cost. Because of God's love, he was satisfied with nothing less than the best. These women of the twenty-first century would say that he loved them so much that nothing else mattered to them. Biblical women would remind the women of today that God loved them so much that everything mattered to him!

E. Sin

God brought about salvation for women of the twenty-first century because it was by his pleasure. He did not do this to please man but for his glory. Because Jesus shed blood on the cross, in him, women had redemption.

With that redemption he afforded them forgiveness. God spread upon women his grace. He had made known his will when he created the heavens and the earth. Salvation was not an act; it was totally the work of the Master.

The fact that women of the twenty-first century did not experience all of the results of sin immediately indicated that God's reign continued in the world after the fall. Did women of the twenty-first century decide what they were meant to be? Was the goal of women of the twenty-first century existence given to them by someone else? It was not blind chance or good luck that accounted for their existence but by the power and purpose of God.

God was opposed to sin and determined to eliminate it from the universe. He was a jealous God and by no means would clear the guilty. There was just no way around it.

F. Salvation

Biblical women would tell women of twenty-first century that salvation was the restoration of God's reign in human affairs. Women of twenty-first century could not imagine how the Apostle Paul felt when he was chosen by the Lord on the Damascus Road. He probably was scared out of his wits. The only way that a person could get to Jesus was if the Father who sent Jesus permitted this.

Women the twenty-first century knew that no one could be saved without actually hearing and responding to the gospel. In other words, Jesus was the source of women of the twenty-first century's salvation. Women could not save themselves. Women of the twenty-first century were the ones that had gotten themselves into that mess (sin) and Jesus was the only one who could get them out of it. If women could be saved without hearing the gospel, what point would it have been to have proclaimed it? God enabled women of the twenty-first century such a powerful incentive—hope!

Often women of the twenty-first century wanted to give up. In some instances the situation appeared hopeless; cancer, physical and emotional abuse, the loss of a child, the addiction, the child that has lost his way, a disease that has stricken the body, the doctor revealed to women that they were dying, the unpaid bills, that motherless child, just to name a few. Because of God's grace, women can look to the hills from whence cometh their help. God sent them *hope*, first class. Then he reminded women of the Holy Spirit that dwelled within them. That same Holy Spirit reminded those women that what they were going through was necessary in order to get them to the next level with God.

MacArthur could not have put it any better when he spoke of the work God has done to make it possible to bring women out of a slave market.[174] God covered them with his grace. Yet, so many times women could not forgive their own sisters and brothers. Women were not worthy!

---

[174] Ephesians 1:13 (NIV).

The women of the twenty-first century's most important actions after being saved were to honor God's authority over every area of their lives and to have given his claims priority over all others. This was one of the first commandments.[175]

Many of those women thought what mattered was women's feelings about God. This was only part of it. What should have mattered was the judgment, a very real source of factual information about what God knew about them.

Women of the Bible would say redemption was possible because of this spirit they call love (bond), between the Father and the Son. He was in women's heart as faith, hope, and love. He set women free to live as his children.

MacArthur Pink's article on Grace Community Church affirmed that the doctrine that proclaimed that God was absolutely sovereign was despised by some. However, women of the Bible would say that without the doctrine, it was impossible to have known God!

G. Conclusion

The Apostle Paul

God equipped Paul so he could immediately begin teaching. This was because although Paul didn't know what had hit him, he knew better than to question God. Paul was trained in Scripture by the Holy Spirit. Women of the Bible were ordained and then sent on their way to do God's work. When the Gentiles got word of this (the Gospel), all of the elect were rejoicing, giving God the highest praise.

MacArthur as well as Pink affirmed that God granted the gift of faith to those whom were elected for salvation. Biblical women would point out that to the chosen; God gave the elect the power to believe. Paul was one of the elect (few) who was chosen before he was born. God chose to use Paul as a vessel because he knew that Paul would not get in the way of his accomplishments. God was glorified and this was why he chose the weak, the despised, and the foolish.

[175] Exodus 20:3 (NIV).

They did not have a problem giving God the glory! Biblical women would ask the women of the twenty-first century if they had a problem giving God the glory.

Paul was on his way to persecute Christians. Biblical women would see that this was hard for many women of the twenty-first century to swallow. However, women of the twenty-first century had not seen what God could do. God the Father drew him, compelled him, pulled him, and then dragged him. Paul had no choice in the matter."[176] Paul did not choose God, God chose Paul! Sin or salvation! Let God be the Judge! This was one of the reasons biblical women instructed women of the twenty-first century to win some unsaved souls to fulfill God's plan. This was God's way of preparing the heart as he stirred the spirit.

[176] John 15:16 (NIV).

GOD GOVERNS

GOD

STIRRED

THE

SPIRIT

CHAPTER 8
God Stirred the Spirit

A. Introduction

The value of the doctrine was where everything rested, according to Arthur W. Pink. It was therefore important that women of the twenty-first century knew that it was because of God's mercy and grace that God had chosen them rather than the choice being the will of that person. Many women of the twenty-first century and of the Bible had never been affirmed for anything in their lives. Women had been unpopular in their communities and in their jobs, just to name a few. However, when women of the twenty-first century walked down that aisle and surrendered their lives to Christ, not by their might, but because it was the inner most core of their being, it was then that they gave their lives to Christ. They had a relationship with God. Women of the Bible would say to women of the twenty-first century that this was why it was important for women of today to work with God. They would appreciate the value of the doctrine.

B. Working with God

Many of these Christian women of the twenty-first century were under the impression that they were working for God; however, they were working with God as he continued to supply their needs. When women of today were working with God, God gave them instructions on what to do, and if they were working for God they had come to the realization that they were limited in what they should do. What did this mean? It simply meant that women had very limited wisdom. God was the author of wisdom. Women of the Bible implied that women of the twenty-first century could do certain things to help others, but God was unlimited in his abilities. It meant that women of the twenty-first century were limited on the ability to love others, but God was love.

C. Free Will

Women of the Bible would point out that free will was not an act of man. So many women of today insisted that free will was regulated by nature. It was Christ who had come to save that which was lost. Women of the twenty-first century relationship with God opened the condition of their hearts with a healing power. It was then that their lives would have been fruitful. Women had yielded to the Spirit. What a Mighty God they serve! Those women had walked in the Spirit. Jesus wanted women to know that his doctrine was not his but that of his Father.

D. Present and Active

God placed biblical women memories into women of the twenty-first century's lives as a source of help and encouragement. God had orchestrated women of the Bible and women of the twenty-first century for his purposes. So many times women of today were not in a spiritual condition to respond because they were in the world rather than being of the world. The Holy Spirit was God himself, present and active, enabling every believer to do whatever God commanded. He would always let them know the Father's will.[177] This was why it was pertinent to keep in mind that God would and did affirm his will for his glory. Biblical women would say that God would not override women's heart, but he influenced their lives toward his will. God's will enabled choices, the immediate cause of women of today's actions. This was why Christ came to do for his people, those incapa-

[177] John 16:13 (NIV).

ble of doing for themselves. Women of the twenty-first century had no power to do good works that were accepting to God without the grace of God! Pride invoked an exaggerated focus on self. One way that women could defeat pride was to focus on God's will and not on women's desires.

E. Conclusion

As the governor among the nation, God had chosen how to guide his people. He pointed them to two relationships: Jesus's relationship to the Father who sent him and his relationship to those God gave him. It was God who controlled every breath that the women of the twenty-first century took and every step that they made. It was God that made women of the twenty-first century disappointments his appointments. It was the relationship that women of the twenty-first century had with God that opened an insight into a condition of their heart and women's dependence on him. God reminded woman of the twenty-first century that his delay did not mean denials, it meant development.

God's provision had already been set for both woman of the Bible and women of the twenty-first century. This helped women to worship the Giver more than the gift. This was why prayer should not be focused on the provision but on his vision. *God* stirred the spirit, being large and in charge.

LARGE

AND

IN

CHARGE

!! ANSWER THE CALL !!

Chapter 9
Large and in Charge

A. Introduction

Women of the twenty-first century wished to inform the woman of the Bible that the God of the universe, the one and only creator of all that was, had continued to call every believer into a special relationship with him. God's call for women of the twenty-first century to have a personal relationship with him was very real. The truth of this was found on almost every page of the Bible. Even more amazing was the knowledge that it was God's choice to call women into a personal relationship with him.

He chose women in him (Christ), before the foundation of the world. Every time a person approached the Bible and opened its pages, he or she aimed face-to-face with the author, God. Biblical women informed women of the twenty-first century that God called individuals into a special relationship with himself to use them to accomplish his purposes. God had everything under control. He called women he could trust to be instruments through which he would accomplish his eternal purposes. Biblical women would say that some of the things women of the twenty-first century could do to win God's trust would be to have daily Bible study and daily prayer time with the Master (God).

B. Taking the Call

Women of the Bible would say that there were times when God searched the world over looking for women of today to use, but may not had found anyone who was willing or living in a way that he could trust them with his work. When God did not have someone who would allow their life to be used, that person had serious consequences. Just think about all of those lost souls waiting to be saved. One example of this was found in Ezekiel.

> "So I sought for a man among them who would make a wall, and stand in the gap before me on behalf of the land, that I should not destroy it, but I found no one. Therefore I have consumed them with the fire of My wrath; and I have recompensed their deeds on their own heads," says the Lord God.[178]

Biblical women say that women of the twenty-first century should not have taken God's call for granted. The Bible made it very clear that women of today would be held accountable. God did not want his people to suffer. God was only asking that people honor him and receive his blessing. The truth applied to every Christian. None were excluded. God had placed women as watchmen, in family life, the workplace, the church, and the neighborhood, to share the good news of God's word. In understanding the call of God in women's lives, it was important to realize that God did not make them for time but for eternity. Women of today knew that God had a plan, and his plan was already set before women of the twenty-first century were thought of by their parents.

---

[178] Ezekiel 22:30–31 (NIV).

C. Redemption

Women of the Bible pointed out to women of today that women knew it was God that redeemed them from sin, forgave them, and then cleansed them. God's call to them were not merely so that women could get to heaven when they died as some may think but so that they could know him, walk with him, serve him from the time of salvation and throughout eternity. God desired a love relationship with women of today because God represented love. God loved women of the twenty-first century before they even knew how to love, drew them to himself, adopted them into his family through this thing they call salvation, and if that wasn't enough, he sent the Holy Spirit to reside in them so that they would have the opportunity to experience and share his love with others. What a Mighty God people serve! Jesus described this love in John 15:9–17. This is why biblical women would want the women of the twenty-first century to take a spiritual inventory of themselves.

D. Spiritual Inventory

One of the things women so often forgot was that they all needed to take a spiritual inventory of their lives in the presence of God. Biblical women would say that God must take women aside regularly to remind them of his call on their lives, bringing to their remembrance all he has said to them, and helping them see how they were responding to his shaping and directing of their lives.

E. Conclusion

Biblical women would say to women of the twenty-first century regular reading of the Bible was when women allowed God to speak to them. Prayer was when women talked to God. Witnessing about his goodness was women's way of sharing God's goodness with others. Prayer brought them into God's presence, where God changed their ways into his ways.

Both women should have kept in mind that without God-given heart, wisdom, understanding, and knowing who Jesus was, was worthless.

Biblical women would say that women of the twenty-first century should love God with all of their hearts, minds, souls, and strength. Women must respond to God unconditionally without hesitation according to biblical women. Biblical women reminded women of the twenty-first century that the Holy Spirit, the enabler, assisted women in hearing, knowing, and answering his call. God was large and in charge, as he continued to take women to that road of eternity.

The Road

To

Eternity

Chapter 10
The Road to Eternity

A. Introduction

Women of the twenty-first century had informed women of the Bible that God was still on the throne. There was no starting point from which women could survey all viable conditions and decide just which would fulfill that God's word had come true. If women of the twenty-first century could do this, they could not be lost; they would have wisdom of God himself. God came to women through the Bible and the church. Women brought nothing to what happened—God did! The human was brought under judgment by the divine.[179]

B. From Man to God

Women of the twenty-first century had decided to take a road that had been opened from God to women. It was impossible to travel along that road in the reverse direction, from woman to God. No activity in this world had value in itself. This value appeared when it became in the medium of obedience to God and women witnessing his glory. Although women of the twenty-first century could not explain the reason God had revealed himself in this way or that way, women should rest assured that he had actually done just that! God was absolute wisdom and his way with women of the twenty-first century should have been without question.

---

[179] John 6 (NIV).

C. God's Claim

God was known only as, and where he chose, in Jesus Christ who was God himself for people's sake. He was under no obligation to make himself known to women. He could have remained forever in his own bliss, had he so willed.

God had a claim upon women of the twenty-first century from which women could not escape, solely because all that women had and all that women knew came from him. Women were bought with a price. God had sustained women's lives. His nature was love, even to those women that were undeserving and rebellious. They all fell short. None of the women were worthy. Women of the twenty-first century would never know how much it cost to see their sins upon the cross. Biblical women would point out that Christ sacrificed his life to save the women of today. What claim upon them for a second was compatible?

All of God's claims were made within the setting of his promise. One example of this was when he promised to leave his covenant, the Holy Spirit. He did just as he promised! Biblical women would point out that God was a man of his word. When women read the Bible, God made it the vehicle of revelation. In him they came face-to-face with God's claim, which was rooted, not in possession of overwhelming might, but in the exercise of his wisdom and his love.

Women of the twenty-first century's attitude toward God should have been one of gratitude. People say, whatever your will is God, but did they really know what they were asking? Women of the Bible warned the women of today to be careful about what they asked from God.

Jesus gave an invitation for unbelievers to accept Christ as their Savior. By nature women of today were slow to move spiritually.[180] They needed encouragement to respond to the offer of the Gospel.

[180] Matthew 4:19; John 1:43–49 (NIV).

D. The Origin of Knowledge

Biblical women warned women of the twenty-first century that God was the origin of knowledge. There was no time when he did not know everything. It would be misleading to speak of God as coming to know something. The Bible told people how God knew what he knew. He knew because he created everything, because he was everywhere, present and in all things. The only reason women of the twenty-first century were where they were was because God ordered their steps. God was still on the throne. Knowledge was one of the gifts God gave them. Paul mentioned a special gift of knowledge.[181]

Women that did not know him or who did not want to come to know him were considered fools. God's revelation to women should have been further analyzed in terms of prophetic, kingly, and priestly functions. God placed people in a situation to learn. He knew what he knew. What greater love than a man that had laid down his life. God caused women of the twenty-first century to know (developmental) and he enabled women to use and apply (application) his word.

E. Conclusion

Women of the twenty-first century should know that God did not give Jesus the authority to throw his weight around. He gave Jesus the authority on earth so that he could give his followers eternal life. Biblical women would say that women of the twenty-first century should have been made aware of the hidden divine past. Women of the Bible could say to today's women that God was the voice that bided those halt that summoned to reckon with their ultimate destiny. Just how many times did God plead his case? Biblical women told women of today that they were not alone! God was still on the throne? Were women of the Bible and women of the twenty-first century connected from the start? The connection was God himself! The road to eternity. This was when the women of the twenty-first century understood the true meaning of God.

[181] Colossians 1:12–18 (NIV).

The

Meaning

Of

God

Chapter 11
The Meaning of God

A. Introduction: God Is/God Reveals

"The Existence of God" seemed to have shifted. In churches, there was confusion and uncertainty about what it meant to speak to God. To have said that God created and sustained the world, that he actively intervened in the affairs of men, and that he had purposed that far surpassed anything women had conceived, raised the question—did women know what they were talking about?

These questions were rising out of a situation of religious pluralism, beliefs in multiple paths to God. Women of the twenty-first century were having a tremendous amount of significance in their own right. God was a mystery, and anything that was said about him was too difficult to prove. This was a problem when trying to identify the intention of God. Women of the Bible were saying women of the twenty-first century should do the will of God. They must first have some way of knowing what God intended. Biblical women would say that women of the twenty-first century would need to have a revelation of God.

B. Revelation

God placed biblical women in women of the twenty-first century lives, revealed his will to women, and then spoke to them in biblical reading. In order for women of today to have had an insight into the will of God, a woman must have had confidence, love, and faith.

Supreme quality with unquestionable integrity must also exist. There was a sense of credibility and a feeling of competence when confronted with a question that may have depicted the existence of God.

C. The Mission

The women of the twenty-first century were on a mission with the Master and by having an intimate, personal, relationship with the Father and the Son; women of the twenty-first century should have been assured that God exists. Women of the Bible had assurance because of God's promise of eternal life, which was knowing God, and being kept by him in a relationship that lasts forever. There was definitely a greater power. God's purpose was to bring women of today into a closer relationship with him. He wanted women of today to repent and to come to a saving knowledge of him.

Did people really know God's will? God was the author of the Book, the Bible. The irony of this was hundreds of years ago the Bible was the first book that slaves learned to read. Women of today knew God's intentions because the Bible was written.

D. His Glory

Women of the Bible were trying to tell the women of the twenty-first century that Jesus wanted his followers to see his glory.[182] Women should finish what God wanted them to do by sharing the Gospel with those for whom Jesus died. Women of the twenty-first century should reveal God's ultimate purpose for them, which was to glorify him. The mission for the women of the twenty-first century should be to focus on what God wanted to accomplish through them, not what women of today wanted to accomplish. It was vital that women of today did what God wanted. Luke stated that David had served God's purpose in his own generation.[183] Women of the twenty-first century's personal mission was serving God's purpose

[182] John 17:24 (NIV).
[183] Acts 13:36 (NIV).

(God's will). Anyone who questioned the existence of God was without wisdom. God chose the elect to tell the world about him. Women of the Bible would probably say to women of the twenty-first century they *should trust God*!

E. Conclusion

Women of the Bible would say, let's reflect to the time when David was delivered from Goliath, the giant, or the time when the three Hebrew boys were cast into the fiery furnace. If those were not enough, what about Jesus walking on water or his controlling the wind? Surely, that was an all-powerful God. The parting of the Red Sea, God's governing of irrational creatures, and his controlling of inanimate matter were all the works of God. God was sovereign. Only God could perform those miracles.

What does this mean? This refers to his supremacy and his primacy. God was above all, in all, and through all. Without a doubt, God was the Alpha and Omega, the beginning and the end. He was the origin of existence, the Creator and Controller of all that they were and all that they have. He was the potter, power over the clay!

Surely, God does exist and his purpose was revealed to women on a regular basis. How did women know this? They knew this because women of the Bible's past informed the women of today. It was important for women of the Bible and women of the twenty-first century to communicate so that this important information revealed the power and existence of God could be passed down through the generations. The Bible revealed that God did exist! God is and God reveals through women of the Bible as well as women of the twenty-first century! He used women of the Bible to speak to women of today so that his will would be accomplished, so that he would be glorified.

Bibliography

Altrock, Chris. *Preaching to the Pluralists: How to Proclaim Christ in a Postmodern Age*. St. Louis, Missouri: Chalice Press, 2004.

Atteberry, Mark. *Free Refill: Coming Back for More of Jesus*. Cincinnati, Ohio: Standard Publishing, 2007.

Coontz, Stephanie. *Marriage, a History: From Obedience to intimacy, or How Love Conquered Marriage*. New York: Viking Penguin Group, 2005.

Crawford, Nancy and Helen M. Devries. *Relationship between Role Perception and Well-Being in Married Female*. http://find.galegroup.com, 2005.

Document Page: "Marriage, Parenthood, Divorce Understanding the Past as We Move." (n.a., n.p., n.d.) http://elibrary.bigchalk.com.

Document. "Perspective on World Christian Movement" (n.a.), 2007. http://find.galegroup.com.

Foltz, Howard. *Healthy Churches in a Sick World*. Longwood, FL: Xulon Press, 2002.

Gaitskell, Deborah. *Gospel Bearers, Gender Barriers*, 2004. http://find.galegroup.com.

Guy-Sheftall, Beverly. *Daughters of Sorrow: Attitudes Toward Black Women, 1880–1920*. New York: Carlson Publishing Co., 1990.

Hagner, Donald. "Postmodern Philosophy" (n.p., n.d.) http://find.galegroupcom, "Postmodern Defined."

Havea, Jione. *Ecumenical Studies*, 547, 2007. httpAnd.galegroup.com.

Higgs, Liz C. *Bad Girls of the Bible*. Colorado Springs: Waterbrook Press Publish, 1973.

Holy Bible. New International Version. Nashville: Holman Bible Publishers, ElectrOhic, 1999.

"How to Start a Cross-Cultural Ministry at Your Church," 2009. http://find.galegroup.com.

httpllelibrary.bigchalk.com.

http: www.politico.com/news/stories/090^{8}/$_{1}$4102.html (n.a., n.p., 2008) http://elibrary:bigchalk.com (Postmodern Defined)

Lockyer, Herbert. *Their Finest Hour*. Old Tappan: Fleming H. Revell Co., 1979.

McCloskey, Liz. "Boys and Girls Together" (n.p., n.d.).

McLaren, Brian. *More Ready Than You Realize*. Grand Rapids, MI: Zondervan, 2002.

Miley, George. *Loving the Church…Blessing the Nations: Pursuing the Role of Local Churches in Global Missions*. Portland: Gabriel, 2003.

Mittelberg, Mark. *Building a Contagious Church*. Grand Rapids: Zondervan, 2001.

Nelson, Alan. *Creating Messaaes That Connect, 10 Secrets of Effective Communications*. Love land, Colorado: 2004. www.grouppublishing.com.

"New Opportunities and Strategies," 2009. http://find.galegroup.com.

Ochs, Vanessa. *Sarah Laughed: Modem Lessons from the Wisdom and Stories of Biblical Women*. NY: Library of Congress Cataloging Data, 2005.

Owens, Virginia Stem. *Daughter of Eve: Women in the Bible Speak to Woman Today*. Colorado Springs: Zondervan Publishing House, 1995.

Pegues, Deborah Smith. *Taming Your Tongue*. Eugene, OR: Harvest House Publishers, 2005.

Phipps, William E. *Assertive Biblical Women*. Westport, CT: Greenwood Press, 1992.

Pink, Arthur W. *The Sovereignty of God*. Grand Rapids: Baker Books, 1984.

Piper, John. *Let the Nations Be Glad*. Grand Rapids: Baker Books, 2003. Questions composed by the writer (Erdie M. Hutchings)

Raver, Miki. *Woman of the Hebrew Bible*. San Francisco: First Chronicle Books LLC paperback edition, 2005.

Root, Michael. "Faith and Order in a Postmodern World." In *Journal of Ecumenical Studies*, 2007. http://elibrary.com

Snyder, Howard. *Global Good News: Mission in a New Context.* Nashville, Abingdon Press, 2001.

Storrs, Landon. "Attacking the Washington (Femmocracy): Antifeminism in the Cold War Campaign against Communists in Government" (Essay)(p. 29, n.d.) hftp://galc group.com.

The Holy Bible. New International Version, Nashville: International Bible Society, 1999.

Twells, Allison. "Congressional Missions and the Making of an Imperial Culture in Nineteenth-century England," 2002. hftp://find.galegroup.com.

Vizenor, Gerald. "Ruins of Representation." http://elibrary.com.

Ward, Ted. "Recent Trends and Baptist Missions," 1999. http://find.galegroup.com.

Warren, Rick. *The Purpose Driven Church.* Grand Rapids: Zondervan, 1995.

Webber, Robert. *Ancient Future Evangelism.* Grand Rapids: Baker Books, 2003.

"What is a People Group?" 2009. http://www.joshuaproject.net.

www.Mayo Clinc.com, Content provided by, updated 2006.

Zackheim, Victoria. *The Other Women.* New York: Warner Books. 2007.

About the Author

Dr. Erdie Mae Roberts Hutchings is the author behind *Women of the Bible vs. Women of the Twenty-First Century*. She is married to William Hutchings Sr., is an educator, a US Army veteran, a minister, a mother of three—William Junior (son), Dr. Yalonda Hutchings MD (daughter), and Brandon Hutchings (son)—and a grandmother of three (Candyce, Micayla, and William Charles). She has now obtained a doctorate in divinity.

As a writer and educator, Dr. Hutchings has her transcript exhibited at a Christian college as guidelines for students pursuing a doctorate degree. Dr. Hutchings' accolades include Rookie Teacher of the Year, City Wide Teacher of the Year, Walmart Teacher of the Year for three years consecutively, STAR Teacher of the Year, and the recipient of Who's Who several times. Her work across multiple disciplines broadly addresses biblical narratives with an emphasis on women of the Bible versus women of today. Her writing also gives insight and inspiration to how women of today view the world through a new lens. In her other life, she is nontiring as she volunteers in the community by feeding the homeless, serving as Sunday school superintendent for eight years, visiting the sick and shut-in, educating seniors, and teaching the Gospel. She loves the Lord, and her favorite scripture is Jeremiah 29:11, "'For I know the plans I have for you,' declares the Lord, 'plans to prosper you and not to harm you, plans to give you a hope and a future.'"

CPSIA information can be obtained
at www.ICGtesting.com
Printed in the USA
LVHW051146011121
702118LV00001B/153

9 781098 062750